THE WAY OF CHANGE

THE WAY OF CHANGE

FINDING JOY IN YOUR JOURNEY

■□■

Hailey D. D. Klein

TUTTLE PUBLISHING
Boston ■ Rutland, VT ■ Tokyo

Permission acknowledgements for use of previously published material are set out on page 183.

First published in 2002 by Journey Editions, an imprint of Periplus Editions (HK) Ltd.,
with editorial offices at 153 Milk Street, Boston, Massachusetts 02109.

Library of Congress Cataloging-in-Publication Data:

Klein, Hailey
    The way of change / by Hailey Klein.-- 1st ed.
      p. cm.
    ISBN 1-58290-032-9
    1. Change (Psychology) I. Title

    BF637.C4 K53 2001
    158.1--dc21   2001038355

Distributed by

USA
Tuttle Publishing
Distribution Center
Airport Industrial Park
364 Innovation Drive
North Clarendon, VT
05759-9436
Tel: (802) 773-8930
Tel: (800) 526-2778

Japan
Tuttle Publishing
RK Building, 2nd floor
2-13-10 Shimo-Meguro
Meguro-Ku, Tokyo,
Japan 153-0064
Tel: 81-35-437-0171
Fax: 81-35-437-0755

Southeast Asia
Berkeley Books Pte. Ltd.
130 Joo Seng Road
#06-01/03 Olivine Building
Singapore 368357
Tel: (65) 280-1330
Fax: (65) 280-6290

First edition
09 08 07 06 05 04 03 02   10 9 8 7 6 5 4 3 2 1

Design by Jill Feron/Feron Design

Printed in the United States of America

■ □ ■

For giving me this day:
Leonora Winn Daniels Klein

TABLE OF CONTENTS

Table of Contents

INTENTION, TRUTH, ACCEPTANCE

Table of Contents

RETURN, RESURRECTION, ASSESSMENT

IN APPRECIATION

There is a proverb that says: "When you stand with the blessings of your mother and God, it matters not who stands against you." In addition to that powerful combination, I stand with friends. I am blessed with many in my life and acknowledge you all with deepest gratitude.

Several folks have been right in the thick of it with me during this particular adventure, and I give many thanks to:

Jessica Warren Bennett, without whom I would be adrift; Marilyn McCabe and Cathleen O'Connell for fact-finding missions and support extraordinaire; Michael Kerber for letting me play on a great team; Scott Manning for the introduction to publishing and to a new friend; Wendy Walsh for unbridled enthusiasm, great stories, and adventures; Darius Petty for all that you helped me believe; Jane Cosner and Sue Blanchard for walks, talks, tea, and clarity; Karin Wood for steadfast friendship; the Goddesses, divine women with me from before the first step; and Ann Marie Almeida for the room to fly and always a safe place to land.

Also appreciation to my family for keeping me close and to John Fadden and Dan Plumley for their generosity of spirit and to all those whoe shared their wonderous stories.

And a grand merci to Jan Johnson, extraordinary editor and friend.

Give me time enough in this place
And I will surely make a beautiful thing.

■ □ ■

from "Mornings Like This"
— Annie Dillard

OVERTURE

■□■□■□■□■□■□■□■□■□■□■□■□■□■□■□■□■■□■

Look—you just initiated change! You picked up this book and now the process is in motion. That was pretty easy, wasn't it? Word is out that there is something in your life or about your life that you want to change or do differently. And we're just getting started. Your actions have power, but so do your thoughts and your emotions. They are all at the root of change and creating all your heart's desire in this life. The momentum of change begins now. It begins simply with the energy of your thoughts and even the words you choose to use. The shift in energy in your mind this minute is all that needs to happen to begin movement. Well, you are still reading, aren't you? You are just changing all over the place. Change is good, change is joy. And don't forget that you have a mighty powerful ally, the universe. You are partners in change because as soon as you show and tell and feel and think out to the universe what you want, you will receive it. When your thoughts, your emotions, and your physical self are all on the same track, then there is nothing to stop you from getting all that you want. We just have to learn how to line everything up together—mind, body, and spirit—and we are ready to go. This journey we are on is about showing up for life every day, whether you feel like standing in the back of the room or leading the brass band up the aisles. Hopefully your bandleader days will increase and the drecky, low-down, hangdog blues days will be outnumbered. Pick the moment and make your move. Show up with all your senses alert and ablaze, ready for adventure.

How we hold people, places, and things in our minds and hearts is enormously powerful. How we hold them in our minds becomes how we hold them in our bodies. That emotional energy can be a source of courage, strength, and wellness or keep us stuck in a place of fear and illness. It is up to us. That energy has to settle somewhere. It can bring us into balance or throw us off track and out of alignment with our higher purpose. Our higher purpose is to live in maximum joy as much as possible, to live passionately, not dreading what comes next but asking, WOW, what comes next?!

■ BEGIN THE BEGUINE ■

You build momentum by first getting the notion of change in your consciousness and then continuing to roll small changes into bigger life changes. The thoughts build with emotions and desire, and the process is carried fully into the attentive world when you speak or shout or sing or whisper your hopes and dreams into the night. The momentum of change picks up and carries itself further, maybe spinning off into another direction or aspect of your life. I am not asking you to jump into making big life changes . . . not yet. It will happen as a result of making your desire link in harmony with your emotional energy and attention or focus. Sneak up on the bigger changes by working toward the small triumphs in parts of your life where you feel courageous and strong. Small shifts and changes are what get the machine fired up.

If you make a shift in one aspect—emotional, spiritual, or physical—the others are impacted as well. Meaningful, lasting change happens when you work on small movements in each area. We will find balance if we direct energy toward our emotional, spiritual, and physical selves evenly. But living in balance means living passionately in all aspects of your life. Peace and quiet isn't the goal. What's the point of peace? Wouldn't you rather wake up every morning excited and curious about the day than with the predominant emotional focus of just getting through it? It is getting "in shape," like anything else, and when it becomes the norm, vs. the occasional, it is easy to maintain. It is not a drain or strain, but the usual. Living passionately does not have to be exhausting; on the contrary, it can be energizing on every front. Living passionately is the process of finding joy in creating the life you want, focusing on life in this very moment, and asking for your heart's desire to come true.

One area of your life cannot become the load-bearing wall, or the whole structure gets pulled down. Spread the energy across the board. Building strength in one area helps us to be courageous and take risks in others. You have to be motivated to question yourself in each aspect of your life. That is why it is important to do physical exercise, to push yourself to face difficult emotional situations, and to question where you fit into the grander spiritual plan. Whether we challenge ourselves physically or open ourselves emotionally or spiritually and let our fears go, we are making room for the sacred to enter. I have had my own doubts and battles with God and religion over the years but am currently nestled in an easier place and have found a way to connect to the Divine that makes sense to me. For me, the Divine is universal energy and needs us as much as we need it to thrive. I ask you to hear my references to God or the Divine however it makes sense to you. And if that means substituting the name of your dog or cat, then that is just fine, because I know how much you love your beasties.

This path is about letting in joy—integrating small changes in your life so that you will have the emotional and spiritual tools to carry through with the bigger changes. Each step you take makes room for the new energy. Creativity is a tool. Awareness is a tool. Faith is a tool. You are supported by the universe, powers so much greater than yourself or the negative voices in your head or from your past, or the fear in your heart. Every strong, courageous, loving thought and gesture refills the well and heals us all.

Working with this book, you will discover your own rhythm of change, open the avenues to allow joy in, and welcome the emotions of change. The first threshold to cross will focus on who you are, how you interact in the world, and how you spend your energy. The second asks you to look at the truth of where you are now as you begin the journey and asks where you want to go. The third invites you to practice with small changes and actions and key in to the momentum you have already been creating. And finally, you will come to a new place as a changed person and will explore what still waits to be done. You will have new tools and emotional vocabulary and also, I hope, a better understanding of your role in your own life. There will be new challenges and questions at every new spot, and you will spin from one place to the next, carrying the momentum and learning to love change and what's around the next corner.

Each step of change is an unfolding, an unfolding that may reveal difficult truths and realizations. The idea is to move past them, drift past them like a balloon in the Macys Thanksgiving Day parade—you can see them as you float on over them, acknowledge them, and keep on going. By all means, don't stay there and get tangled up in the wires. Understanding and accepting these truths and realizations will carry you on to the next step of the journey and closer to lasting change by making room for courage and joy. If you follow through the steps and cross each threshold, you will gain a better understanding of the energy within and around you and, therefore, the power to influence the momentum of change.

My grandmother was a recognized collage artist who came to it when she was in her fifties. When I was young, she set me up at my own little table while she was working and gave me my own supplies to create with. One of her sisters was a painter, another a singer, and their mother was a dancer and activist—creativity runs deep in the family. I have fallen into writing in my thirties and seem to write like I make collages. Come to think of it, this is how I make quilts and cook, too. First there is a wild flurry of tearing and shouting and crashing and then flipping through piles of paper and magazines and bits of boxes and bags. Then, by trying little things here, throwing paint and sparkles at the paper there, and then obscuring almost all of what I just put down with seven more layers of color and texture just because something else caught my eye, something is hatched. My friend Cathleen likens me to a raccoon because they are intrigued by shiny things and I can't seem to stay on one subject for more than a very few minutes. I, too, am distracted by shiny things. I am not great at structure or confined spaces, so that is what you get with my writing style, too. Let's think of it as a collage. There may be interesting corners and sections that reveal themselves over time and after several passes. I hope the overall canvas is pleasing and maybe intriguing and inspiring. The adventure of life is textured, layered, colorful, and ever-changing. And that is a good thing.

I wrote *The Way of Change* as a journey of discussion and discovery about ourselves, our energy, and the energy all around us, and how we can impact change in our lives and in the world. There is great work to be done and challenges to be met in the stillness as well. For some, the quiet will be the hardest part—not only making room for it but looking at and accepting what you may find there. A day away from a workout is when muscles are built in physical training, and the same can be said for the stillness in spiritual training. The exercises focused on delving into a spiritual assessment are as important as any action steps. If you are focused on every worst-case scenario, disease prevention instead of wellness as the natural state of being, letting fear and unhappiness predominate, then we will work to change your emotional vocabulary. We will work to make joy and possibility predominate your thoughts and emotions and be the stars in your spiritual theater.

We will explore fear, but only in passing, because I don't want you to stay there. Through stories and exercises, we will look at how faith, intuition, and spirit are involved with changing our lives. Some of the exercises just might bring up the questions you were hoping would go away or truths you have turned away from. We've all done that. Following through with the exercises builds consciousness through the shift, and using new or atrophied emotions helps trigger the momentum of change. Sometimes the best we can do is to just figure out the questions and take small, deliberate steps as an answer, and that is the best place to begin. We know all these answers already of what brings us joy and how we want our lives to be, but we may have to quiet the noise that has drowned these voices out. We will reach inside to bring out the thoughts that bring us maximum joy and begin the journey leading with these emotions for a change.

You may balk at certain steps in the process and have to repeat others before you are ready to move further along. Take this on in your own time, at your own speed. We all learn differently. It may be challenging at first, and uncomfortable, and probably unfamiliar. Part of the challenge is to stay there and not fall back into the familiar. It is easier to go from a place of pain to a place of joy than to go from a place of complacency to a place of joy. From complacency we tend to sink into fear and unhappiness, rather than making the leap to euphoria. The tasks and assignments are designed for you to create subtle energy shifts and to refocus emotional cues to carry you through. Hopefully, you will integrate some of them into your life permanently. You may need to learn to walk again when you just got used to running everywhere, but when you begin to feel the momentum of change, you will feel the power of the energy within and around you. You will be amazed. And that is the point of life, after all.

■ CH-CH-CHANGES ■

Many women I know, including myself, react the same way to dramatic (or traumatic) change in our lives—we cut and/or dye our hair. I am certain I do it as a catalyst for change. It's so immediate and doesn't take months or years, like dieting or learning French. I'm known as the "woman of a thousand hairstyles" by my friend David because every time he sees me, my hair is different. Somehow telling myself, "It is only hair, it will grow back," gives me permission to change other aspects of my life and slip into other personas. Sometimes I find the motivation and courage to venture into the unknown, the untried territories of spiritual discovery. Small changes are a good way to begin. If a small external change is going to inspire you to make courageous internal changes, then take that small bite and see what happens.

My hair has gotten pretty short since I began writing this book. It has been a joyful and challenging journey. I believe what I have written with all of my heart. I offer it with the intention of inspiring you to act with grace as often as you can and to find joy on the journey you are on now or the new path yet to be discovered, yet to be embraced.

I urge you to accept both the missteps and the triumphs on your journey. In doing so, you may reveal your personal source springs of courage. You may become more mindful of the world around you, stay longer in a place of joy and wonder, and find a deeper gratitude for all that is present and possible in your life. Take away what inspires you and leave what doesn't. Through the many stories I tell in the book, you may find the world a little bit smaller; you just might feel reassured to know that you are not alone with your questions, reactions, or dreams. Better yet, my hope is that they will inspire you on your journey of self-discovery. Through working with this book, may you discover what ignites your spirit.

P.S. You will come across quotes from writers, poets, and inspirational voices throughout the book. Read all the quotes out loud when you come across them, even if you have read/heard them before. You may hear something you didn't allow through your filters last time, so listen between the lines. Read each line slowly, digest it, roll around in it, dance on it. You will likely hear something for the first time.

■ THE HARD PARTS DISCUSSION ■

Significant change of any kind requires looking inward and understanding the energy of where we are and who we are. You are the only one who can change your life. I repeat: You are the only one who can change your life. No program, book, or seminar does it for you. The process of change begins the very moment you think about something differently. Some of the steps toward change are emotionally challenging and involve time, thought, and action. It may take you longer to work through some stages than others. You will meet resistance at every step, from yourself and from others close by in your world. It is hard enough to deal with your own fears without absorbing other people's, too. You will have to take extra care not to let other folks derail you on your journey. Remember how far you have come by focusing on the desire for change; things are already in motion. I will try to provide tools along the way, but you will have to do the hard parts. Allowing can be a hard part, at first. Sometimes it may seem difficult just to water the plants, greet the sunrise, or walk the dog, but these simple activities are the place to begin practicing to notice, to appreciate, and to do so passionately—every cell in your body will respond to these feelings of joy.

■ GETTING OUT OF THE WAY ■

Poet Rainer Maria Rilke wrote about transforming joy from within for the most significant impact. Transforming joy within does not mean blindly jumping right into the action phase of change, but looking before we leap—understanding the authentic needs and desires for change and our motivations for initiating the movement, then getting ourselves out of the way, and just sitting back and letting it happen. We do need to be at peace with where we must begin, which is at the truth.

We are the only ones in the way of getting everything that we want and having a joyful, abundant life. It may be easier to assign blame to everyone who ever made an appearance in your life, but every day, all day, we make decisions with information we experience. We decide not only how to physically respond to people, places, and things but how to respond emotionally and spiritually. We may or may not be conscious of how we are responding. If we are conscious of what kind of energy we are directing at someone or something, it may be a learned, self-conditioned response that does not get us anywhere but into an emotional rut. We have the choice to respond differently each and every time.

The universe will respond to movement or change, no matter how small, conscious or unconscious. It has to, for energy shifts of any size are met with a response—action, reaction. One change in the system changes the whole system itself. Not only will you be different at the end of the new road, but your immediate and the greater universes will be altered along with you. Effortless turnarounds do not exist at this level of spiritual transformation, however. This is the hardest work you will ever do. Once you find your new rhythm, though, you can flow through life with greater ease with tools to cut yourself free from the brambles if you get caught up.

■ REMEMBERING HOW TO WALK ■

There is good reason why most of us cannot succeed with the all-action-oriented "just do it" attitude: it sets us up to fail. Overnight, dramatic change is usually fleeting. You can't wake up and say to yourself, "I am going to go out and run ten miles today," if you haven't moved off the couch in six years. Well, you can say it, but I am not sure how far you will actually get. You can't run ahead of yourself emotionally, either. "I will never say a mean thing about anyone, and I will definitely never eat another cookie so long as I live." You are just setting yourself up for disappointment with that approach. If you ignore the emotional and spiritual steps, the change will have nothing to anchor itself to, nothing more than vapor. This is a training or retraining process. Micromovements in focus and emphasis are all that are required. I learned that on a physical plane in yoga class. Micromovements have a tremendous impact on the whole experience. The physical carries over into the emotional and spiritual realms in yoga, and that is true in life as well.

■ I Don't Know How They Keep Finding Me ■

This may sound like a familiar story. Don't stop reading if you have heard it or lived it before. Read it again just to make sure. After being lied to and cheated on and taken advantage of for several years, a friend of mine left a bad relationship. This was a good final move after several false starts. Her response was to change everything externally in her life. She moved, found a new job, and dyed her hair. Great! None of these are bad to do, but neither an assessment nor an understanding of her role in the relationship was ever addressed in the process. Almost instantly she was involved with a new man. Although he was not abusive, she discovered early on that she was playing the exact subservient role she had in the abusive relationship. Her new answer was that it must be that there are no good men out there. Not fair. Nothing had changed because she hadn't looked inside to see where this attraction and behavior was coming from. She was overlooking her role in the situations. She was attracting the same circumstances and relationships over and over again. Behavior patterns are broken only if we look at our own role in perpetuating them. Learn to recognize familiar situations and emotions. Ask yourself how you feel. If it doesn't feel right at your core, then it isn't. When we understand where we have focused our emotional energy, consciously and unconsciously, then we can decide to do things differently today, right this minute. And not just decide but know it, and connect to that decision with our hearts and minds and spirits that we want something different. This is the understanding and internalizing step to meaningful change. Life doesn't just happen to us. We have a role in it. We are conducting the symphony, and wherever we point our baton, that instrument/emotion is emphasized or spotlighted. We forget that we can redirect the emphasis at any time. When the whole orchestra is playing in harmony and rhythm, with lovely solos here and there, is there anything better? Either we allow it to happen and impact us a certain way or we influence and redirect it.

■ LOOK WHAT I MADE! ■

Here we are on this magical journey and we have the chance to change everything about it all day, every day, with every decision we make and thought we think and emotion we attach to each choice—all that we offer into the world. Change involves courage, truth, and faith. Change does not mean instant cure or happiness, because each alteration, however small, brings with it its own set of lessons and challenges. It requires listening to and hearing yourself and others without filters. Let your critical voices fade away, and live more consciously in the realm of all things possible. Change is challenging and happens whether or not we consciously decide to influence it, so we might as well hop on that bad-boy freight train and see if we can fling ourselves off near the stop we want. Remember when you were little and you made some spectacular glittering piece of art and ran through the house to show someone, shouting, "Look what I made!" That is joy. That is this life.

TOOLS FOR THE JOURNEY

■□■□■□■□■□■□■□■□■□■□■□■□■□■□□■

What you are embarking on is really a journey, a journey within the grander one of life. Along the way you may encounter surprises, frustrations, newfound emotions, and, hopefully, great joy. You carry with you at all times a bag of tricks that you may just need reminding of as you set off. The tools are handy and access to them is just a thought away. It is always a good idea to travel with tools and supplies if you are going on a journey—you know, just in case you get stuck in the mud, find yourself lost, or eat bad road food. Three convenient tools when traveling down a path of energy shifts and change are: creativity, faith, and connection. Use these tools throughout your journey, as touchstones or reminders of the spiritual and emotional resources available to you.

■ CREATIVITY ■

Creativity appears like fireflies—blink, the light is there; blink, it is gone. It may only be inklings of new ways of looking at your world, but accessing creative energy is as easy as planning a meal, taking a new route to work, or painting a door in your living space red just because you love the color.

This journey we're on together is also meant to unlock the creative gifts you were born with. We are all creative, each and every one of us. Sometimes we may just need reminders. Being creative is not necessarily the same as being artistic. Try to let go of any "results-oriented" focus you may hold inside in connection with being creative. Being creative doesn't mean you have to produce a beautiful picture or sculpture when the bell rings and time is up. Try to let go of the associations with scissors, paint, and paper, if they are lingering nearby in your consciousness. Being creative can quite simply mean looking at a familiar landscape or even a problem in a new way. Some of the most wildly creative folks I know do not make art for a living. They just can't help being creative. It is just as involuntary as taking a breath. Thinking and acting creatively can be learned. My friend Wendy Walsh gives her students this Abraham Maslow quote: "People who are only good with hammers, see every problem as a nail." How brilliant is that? This woman met her future husband on an airport bus and fell in love with him after saying yes to his invitation to Nepal. Don't forget to ask the question and extend the invitation, and don't forget to say yes. As another friend of mine says, "Instead of a quick no, how about a slow yes?" Try lots of different tools, not just hammers. Use them in combinations, turn them upside down, and use them backwards. You can't imagine how much fun it is to break the rules.

We are creative all day, every day, in our problem solving and interactions. Creativity is not product- or end-result dependent, as many may have been lead to believe. Every situation we encounter requires some degree of right-brain activity. Organizing your closet is creative. Finding a way to handle a difficult confrontation is creative. Talking to children is creative. Creativity is the process, the experimenting, and the pushing oneself outside of the routine ways of being in the world. Don't get hung up on the outcome. I am talking to you Type A personalities. So, this quote by Donald Kennedy is for you:

A lot of disappointed people have been left standing on the street corner waiting for the bus marked "perfection."

Thinking creatively gives us freedom, more room to move around in the universe. Acting creatively means breaking free of rigidity, coloring outside the lines. We may start to see the world differently and be in the world differently. The world becomes bigger, and the possibilities may seem limitless. Creativity has some risk involved, more like a happy challenge. I agree with abstract artist Helen Frankenthaler when she claimed, "I'd rather risk an ugly surprise than rely on things I know I can do." Try something new, push yourself to feel the good fear, the fear that if you push through, it will make you exponentially stronger and a much more interesting human.

Creative inspiration comes from everywhere and sometimes out of nowhere. The fireflies blink their mighty little lights right outside the window and you can't help but notice and wonder. You don't want to catch them and put them in a jar, or they might die. You want to watch them for a while and see what happens. Creative thoughts happen like that. They can appear in your dreams or be inspired by a song on the radio, the colors in a room, or the clouds on the horizon. Mostly you just have to pay attention to the hints and inklings of inspiration all around you.

FREE-RANGE CHICKEN CREATIVITY

My friend Greg is an inspired cinematographer and musician. He most definitely lives a pan-creative life. He is a natural-born creative. Greg felt as if he had no other choice but to live a creative life. It is who he is. It was a burden when he was young to be told constantly, "Oh, Greg, you are so creative," when he didn't even know what that meant yet. He told me that later on he came to realize that maybe it meant he saw, heard, or experienced the world differently than other people. His mission became a journey to connect with like-minded folks to work and spend time with. At the risk of sounding born-again, Greg says that his creativity springs from "abandon, risk, and ultimately surrender." He describes creative people as generally "thoughtfully, presently absent," their minds drawing on past and future stimulation with influences flying in from everywhere. Greg thinks about it in terms of parameters and what he calls "free-range chicken creativity." He said that unlike chickens, he needs some boundaries to his roaming in order to be content and at his best. If someone tells him to go shoot a scene the way he wants, for instance, with no clear direction, he feels as if he has too much wide-open space in the creative landscape. If, on the other hand, they tell him to shoot a scene to invoke the bleakest, most rainy day in London using only a gray palette but giving the slightest hint that the weather and mood may clear, well, then he has his parameters, and his creativity is unleashed and can run wild. Give yourself some parameters if the open range seems too vast, but don't lock yourself in the chicken coop and refuse to come out.

I admit that I didn't often read the poetry in *The New Yorker* until recently. I always read the cartoons. Well, I did read Sharon Olds's and Mary Oliver's poetry, which generally sets a spark or rocks a musical nerve. Once I saw their work there, I realized I had better take a closer look. Some hidden gems and inspiration may be lurking inside. You can never be sure where you will find creative inspiration, so keep your receptors open. It may hit you while you are dreaming, driving, or taking out the trash. Something or someone may be that ember that you can't ignore. The idea, already in our subconscious, comes flying to the surface and we recognize it as it appears. A connection is made and our brain cells jump to attention, our fingers twitch, and a stirring down deep begins.

Don't forget to write down ideas and inspirations, sing them, or dance them. Do something to act on them because they seem to disappear as fast as they arrive. I have scraps of paper and note cards in my car, by my bed, and tucked into books and journals and everywhere. Some of them have just a word or a line written on them. I never know how or when they will inspire me, but eventually they always do. We can have amazingly vivid dreams and remember them in the first few groggy moments of our waking, only to find all memory of them gone in the next seconds. Record it somehow. The information is significant. You might not know why immediately, so just let it be.

There are even workshops given in several places across the country that address accessing your creativity if you need an extra boost. Try one if you want. It would probably be great fun. My friend Wendy (remember, from the airport bus and the hammers?) is a photojournalist who teaches a class called "Learning to See." She encourages her students to think differently about the process of making pictures. She reassures them that the technical information about photography can be learned, but each one of them will see and photograph the world differently. Wendy infuses them with the notion that their vision and perspective is truly unique. She gives her class the assignment of photographing a roll of toilet paper. Finding beauty in the mundane is creativity at its best. She encourages them (and me) to be curious and ask questions, especially "What if . . . ?" and "Why not . . . ?" Here is one of my favorite quotes she gives to her class. It is by the late designer Tibor Kalman:

The perfect state of creative bliss is having power (you are 50) and knowing nothing (you are 9).

I actually think we are more powerful and know everything at age nine because we tend to be so much more open to the possibilities in the world, but I understand what he is saying. I fall somewhere in between nine and fifty on the time line, but I have learned to learn again by just allowing. It is so fun to feel nine years old again. Try it.

Tap into your creative energy. Ask, "What if . . . ?" of a problem or just let yourself explore colors and textures and shapes in the world.

Peonies, their scent and craggy pinkness, always remind me of my grand-mother, and that makes me smile and get motivated, for she was an artist. Visits to her house in the very early spring meant big earthenware bowls full of paperwhites in the living room, their dynamic aroma greeting you eagerly as you entered the front hall.

Dodo (a nickname her brother had given her that stuck from childhood) had extensive flower gardens and worked in them every day in the summer. Fresh flowers filled the house. Ironically, my grandmother had no sense of smell. She lost it as a result of illness when she was young, yet she loved beau-tiful things around her and what she remembered as beautiful-smelling things. Today, even a single peony in a mason jar on my desk settles me into a creative space.

■ FAITH ■

Faith is not the same as believing. Faith is knowing and not knowing at the same time. Indian poet and philosopher Rabindranath Tagore captured the essence of true faith when he wrote, "Faith is the bird that feels the light and sings when the dawn is still dark." Faith is the fine line between sheer terror and a sigh of relief. Faith is a knowingness, a connection to and acceptance of the idea that we need to show up every day and say, "I am here and I am ready." The not knowing is the wondrous pilgrimages and all of the passion-ate questions. It is the understanding that the world does not revolve around us but that we are just one tiny part of the glorious whole. I would not presume to tell you what or whom to believe in—that is your job to discover. Faith, like prayer, is a dialogue. It emanates from journeys and inquiries.

Finding faith isn't something to be sanctimonious about, just like being a vegetarian doesn't make you a better person. Just as soon as you start feeling a little bit smug and think you have done all the work and have faith all figured out, I promise you something will happen to rattle you to the core. You will be spiritually slammed into next week and knocked off your feet. If there are any rules to the game, that is rule number one. Faith is a constant and fluid challenge. The universe will never cease in testing our faith. It is part of the package, part of the plan. The harder we struggle against that, the more tests we are likely to encounter, or at least the harder they may appear to us. Finding your faith will make it just a bit more peaceful. Faith gives us more ingredients for our big ol' humble pie—awe and acceptance.

At the beginning of her lovely book, *Traveling Mercies*, Anne Lamott talks about her experience of finding faith:

> *My coming to faith did not start with a leap but rather a series of staggers from what seemed like one place to another. Like lily pads, round and green, these places summoned and then held me up while I grew.*

You will be held up and supported on your journey, sometimes in ways that might not make sense at the time. Tests of faith and courage provide us with strength for the next go-round of challenges. Roadblocks and traumas will also appear in every physical and emotional way, shape, or form. Faith asks that you whisper into the still, dark night, "Okay, I am listening. I'm pretty afraid, but I am listening."

The initiation of movement is the leap of faith, the stepping into the fire, clutching onto an armful of fear that wonders if you might drown—enough fear to be aware—but a transcendence of that fear allows you to take the steps. We are momentarily alone and vulnerable spiritually, and this is a great challenge, but we must take this courageous flight in order to make a space for grace and transformation. It is when we must key in to our faith, not necessarily our beliefs but the essence of true faith, a knowing and at the same time not knowing. Initiation is spiritual thrill seeking in all its glory, an emotional risk taking. St. John of the Cross, a sixteenth-century theologian, writes beautifully about such experiences in high contemplation:

> *I entered into unknowing,*
> *yet when I saw myself there,*
> *without knowing where I was,*
> *I understood great things;*
> *I will not say what I felt*
> *For I remained in unknowing*
> *Transcending all knowledge*

Faith is what gets us through and pushes us to the other side of the hard parts. Faith is electric and holds amazing energy if we choose to explore it. Try being the bird and sing into the darkness.

■ CONNECTION ■

Energy connects us to people and places and the universe. Connections can bring us peace and strength. Connections can reassure us that we belong somehow and somewhere. We become aware of our links to and part in the grandly textured physical and spiritual landscape. I imagine this may be one of the motivations for the surge in the number of people exploring alternative energy work like Reiki, polarity, cranial sacral, and other practices. We wonder how we fit in to the bigger picture and how all the puzzle pieces fit together. I don't believe we need concrete answers, just glimmers and suggestions. In our technology-oriented world we are becoming more disconnected from one another and nature. We can't be a champion of either unless we stay connected.

A person entering a room can dramatically influence the energy. Aren't there people you know who just make you want to be around them, their energy is so warm and inviting? I will sometimes try to engage strangers with good energy in conversation, connect with them. The energy exchange feeds my spiritual curiosity and hunger and hopefully the other person's, too. Sometimes, if I am receptive, it even brings clarity to something I've been struggling with. Remaining responsibly open to the good energy out there makes the universe seem full of wonder and all possibilities limitless. You may be surprised to suddenly meet someone who helps you find the answers you have been searching for. Come to expect it. There are no accidents, and people come into our lives because we have attracted them. They are here for a reason.

I am not advocating striking up conversations with absolutely everyone you encounter or forging relationships instantly. A meaningful connection can be as simple as smiling, opening your eyes, or listening. Beware of energy leeches in the world—the ones who latch on and suck you dry without replenishing your energy stores. If you allow them into your life, they will not leave until you not only ask them but believe yourself that is what you want. You won't attract them into your life if your emotions and energy are clear and in line. Some seeker leeches don't know that they do this, and others may be sly enough to know exactly what they are doing. All relationships in the universe are reciprocal. They may be lopsided at times, but the point is that they even out at some point. Your intuitive radar will speak to you about people as well as places, so make sure you pay attention. When you give all of yourself away to other people's problems and energy requirements, not only is there nothing left for you, but you are hiding and denying yourself your own desires. Let your own light shine.

When we live consciously, we can recognize our own power as that given in connection with all things greater than ourselves. By being conscious in every sense and with every sense, we can create sacred space around us every day and everywhere. Creating sacred space grounds us in the present and assures us of our place in the world. Sacred spaces, the open moments, tiny cracks in the time continuum when we leave all spiritual, psychological, and sociological obstacles behind us, lower walls and invite abundance and wonder in. By recognizing and remembering joy, we create sacred spaces. Creating sacred spaces changes our relationship to the hour and the day, to ourselves, to others, and to the universe. We observe the extraordinary in the everyday and are humbled and reborn.

We create sacred space by inviting others in, letting down boundaries, and letting go of fear. Sacred space is created when we make eye contact with our fellow man and woman on the street, no longer strangers but fellow travelers we have invited into our immediate universe. It is connections between people, intimacy at its height, acknowledgment of another's existence, bonding us together now in this time and place. Sacred space is that fleeting speck of worldly time and connection that exists between a father and daughter, as when my four year-old niece suddenly stops walking to urgently whisper a secret into her father's ear—fleeting in time but everlasting in spirit and connection.

AWAKENING SPIRITUAL CONNECTIONS

Regina Sara Ryan describes in her fine book, *The Woman Awake: Feminine Wisdom for Spiritual Life*, her reaction to experiencing Janis Joplin perform for the first time, illustrating the power and glory of music from the soul:

When Janis sang the blues, she stabbed you with the suffering of humanity, and you felt your own suffering. I wept for completely selfish reasons. With each uninhibited rendering of song after song, I felt more acutely and bitterly my own inability and unwillingness to swing out, open up, "tell it like it is" in my art and work. I wept for my smallness of heart and for the thousand daily choices to make life comfortable rather than leave it somewhat raw, clumsy, open-ended and rife with possibility.

Connecting to dormant or hidden passions in our soul can give rise to great inspiration. We forget to look at what lies within and we forget how to awaken what is sleeping there. Music and dance and art are means to use to connect to parts of us that we don't often reveal. Turn that car radio up high and sing at the top of your lungs. Dance with your partner in the kitchen before dinner tonight. Pull out photos from long ago and study the faces. Remember how you feel.

HONORING MEMORIES

Honoring memories by giving them space in your heart is another way of connecting. The tactile, the ephemeral, dreams, sounds, and aromas that transport us to other times, places, and planes of consciousness; they are the memories of those we have known, places we have been, adventures we have dared. Memories house our fears, our sadness, and our rapture.

How are you connected in this world? What is your history? Where do you get your strength, your commitment, your talents, your hazel eyes, and your aversion to orange food? What people, relatives, or friends impacted your life growing up? How? Describe some of your most vivid memories. Do you remember any little details of the scenes? How do you think they have influenced you and decisions you have made? Who is influencing you now? Our family or tribal connections can be complicated, but for better or for worse, it is how we receive our early information about life and how to live.

I remember piling into my grandfather Bud's green Mustang convertible with my sister and brother on summer nights when we were young and it stayed light until bedtime. We climbed in with our pajamas on, and he would drive around with the three of us squished in the backseat. I was usually in the middle, and we would lean our heads way back and watch the sky blur by. I don't remember any sounds except the trees in the wind. We all stayed very quiet. It is a memory that takes me right back to the moment, and even when it was happening I was nowhere else but right there as the landscape melted around me. It was a time of few worries, when most things were bigger than us but in a free and wonderful way. Memories are elusive phantoms and we all store them away differently, but this is one I carry with me always. My brother and sister may hold it as a part of their stories in other ways, but it is there somewhere, just the same.

THE GODDESSES

I belong to a women's group. We call ourselves the Goddesses—no disrespect or undue vanity intended. I don't even remember just how the name came about. We have been getting together faithfully once a month for six years for dinner, laughter, conversation, and the chance just to be women for a few moments. Once a year or so we sneak away for a weekend to spend time outdoors at the ocean or in the woods. It isn't always easy for spouses and partners to understand the need we have for one another, the strength we gain from our connection and simply being together. We come back to them transformed each time, our spirits renewed, our wells refilled. One goddess's husband loves it when she has a weekend with the group because she always returns with a passionate appetite.

We are artists, writers, businesswomen, teachers, mothers, wives, daughters, partners; married, divorced, single; employers, employees, and self-employed. We are thirty-something, forty-something and fifty-something—outdoorsy, indoorsy, dramatic, and shy. But when we come together each month, we are women. We need no other title. It is a refuge from expectations. It is the glory of no-strings-attached connecting with acceptance and love.

Each of us in the group has been lovingly carried through bumpy times. We have been mentored, cajoled, and lauded through brave change, confusion, new relationships, grief, loss, and triumph alike. The energy created by our connection is tremendous. We often joke that the estrogen levels in spaces we occupy could take out a small army. I realize that this kind of group is not for everyone and there are other ways to make connections. Some women have come and stayed, others have moved away for work, life, and love. Still others have sniffed around a little and moved on, not finding what they needed or not arriving at the right time.

Making connections with others isn't always easy. We are thrown together with peers at an early age, and that continues through school. We are then on our own to find people we like and who like us, people we connect with. Sometimes even now when I am making a new friend I feel as though I am eight years old again. I am hoping I will get invited to the "cool girls'" slumber party because they want to invite me, not because their mom is making them.

There is risk involved with opening up yourself to reveal fears and vulnerabilities, to connecting at our sources of truth. Terry Tempest Williams writes when talking about the idea of exposing our true selves that "we commit our vulnerabilities not to fear but to courage. . . ." Find or rediscover powerful connections in your life. Find a safe place to ask questions and test emerging emotions and fears. It is thoroughly reassuring to speak your truth and see heads bob in understanding of what you are saying. The words "I know just what you mean, I feel the same way" will liberate you when they are said to you. Make time in your life and space in your heart for connecting with others. Embrace it wholly with the most terrified, tentative parts of your spirit. The rewards are limitless, the power immense.

Someday after mastering the winds, the waves,
the tides, and gravity, we shall harness—for God—
the energies of love. And then, for the second time
in the history of the world, man will have discovered fire.

■ □ ■

from *Les Directions de l'Avenir (Towards the Future)*
—Pierre Teilhard de Chardin

ENERGY

■□■□■□■□■□■□■□■□■□■□■□■□■□■□■□■□■□■

A discussion of energy is in order at the outset because it is key to discovering the entrance to the garden. Everything and everyone and everywhere has energy. We ourselves are indeed energy, and energy or life force is all around us, in our thoughts and emotions. We just need to remember. We feel it in our bellies, our intuitive selves, in our very centers. Too often we dwell in our heads, relying on our analytical hemisphere rather than listening to the information coming from our source of intuition, our source of true self. Don't underestimate energy's existence as an entity. Have the courage to recognize and respect it. Every cell in our bodies holds the emotional energy of our thoughts and actions. This impacts our health and our happiness.

Anytime you do something new and challenging, whether it is just making the decision or taking the step, you are influencing energy, aligning yourself with rhythms of the universe, the rhythms of your internal self. The collective unconscious, generally not words spoken aloud but thoughts and desires and preoccupations, shows the power of thoughts generated in our hearts and souls, not just our minds. The words spoken only on the inside carry great energy out into the world. You can change the energy around people and events simply by how you choose to be or respond to what they put out to you. Hair-trigger responses to familiar situations can become a routine and keep you stuck spinning your energy wheels—putting out the same energy in response and never getting a different reaction or moving around the obstacle yourself. If you change the way you respond to the people around you, those people in turn will have no choice but to respond differently to you. That is a key to understanding what using energy is all about. If you change the way you think and actually feel about a situation, then you change the way you respond to the same circumstances if they appear again. You can only control how you respond, and that in turn will make changes in other people's responses. Once those changes have been made, you cannot return to the place as it was before, but you will have set in motion another set of stimuli to react to and make decisions about. You will also likely attract new players to the scene who will add new dimensions as joyous or possibly challenging additions.

■ PLACE ENERGY ■

Energy is all around us all the time. It sneaks into corners and builds nests in cupboards and under chairs. It will wrap around your head and settle into your pockets. It can hit you full-on like a storm, swirling and moving and overwhelming. In any space, every experience, both joyous and difficult, whispered or shouted, that took place there collects and creeps out into our field of recognition, seeking to settle in either our consciousness or subconsciousness. We cannot help but notice, but we can unwisely choose to disregard what we sense. Keying in to the energy in spaces is a great way to begin to understand and experience energy in our lives.

Have you ever walked into rooms or spaces and felt either very uncomfortable or immediately at ease? Places where you can't wait to flee from? And then others you feel like settling in to and staying forever? It isn't easy to pinpoint or explain why, just a feeling in the pit of your stomach. In fact, you may have to battle the practical, analytical messages coming from your head telling you to ignore those feelings. And whether or not spaces are full of people or empty, the energy in the space is what you will pick up on and pay attention to. Any space is never truly empty energetically. You just have to listen from your inside. This is your intuitive voice speaking, and it hates to be ignored.

■ THE UGLY HOUSE ■

Perfect timing: my friend Claire in Seattle just called to say that she and her husband, Ben, are in negotiations for a house that they realize they don't really like. Not only is it ugly, she said, but it just doesn't *feel* right. I told her to run, not walk, away from the deal. Her intuition is screaming at her that this is not the house for them. Her practical brain is trying to out shout her intuition: "Well, it *is* in a good neighborhood," and "Maybe we won't find anything else." Wrong and wrong again. As I told her, "You cannot buy a house you do not love or at least see the lovable qualities hidden under the ugliness."

It makes no sense to buy a house that you refer to in your head as "the ugly house." Ben and Claire won't be able to change their feelings about the house with that kind of energy directed at it all the time. The easy part is that they both reacted the same way, so now they don't have to argue about it. Now they need faith that the right house or situation is out there for them and will materialize. It will all be fine as long as they listen to what is being relayed via their intuitive selves. The minute you do not listen to your intuition you *will* make a mistake. That applies to everything, not just real estate.

Flash forward to several months later: Claire and Ben found a house they loved AND they went against the advice of their real estate agent and several friends because they loved the house so much. They are all moved in and are very happy where they landed. The new house requires some work, but they will make the space their own.

Energy of places and spaces is energy we can identify, and that same energy is within and all around us. In the quiet we can find it and ally with it, partner with the universe to create change and maximize the joy flowing in to our lives. Identifying energy is embracing the unfolding and keying in to the rhythm of change. You cannot totally control how things are going to happen or how people will react to you. You have to be flexible, or you might just miss the most important information. You can make a plan but then should plan on being surprised, along the way and at the outcome. My friend Sue loves the mountains and the woods. Many years ago she found a picture of a cabin in a forest that struck her as the perfect getaway spot. She kept the picture with her over the years, putting out her intention of attracting the scene in the picture into her world. She moved several times, living in Texas and Colorado and then on the East Coast. Sue missed the big mountains and wide-open spaces of the West, but wasn't she surprised to meet a man with a cabin in the mountains of a different state. It was the exact cabin from the picture. It didn't happen the way she thought it would, or in the place she envisioned, but there it was. Be open to what shows up in your life. You brought it into your world and you can welcome it or ask for something else. Your desires will always be delivered to you. The more surprised you are at what arrives may be an indication of how out of touch you are with your emotional/spiritual reality and where your energy is actually mostly focused.

Just like those group trust exercises where you allow yourself to fall back and trust everyone will catch you, that is how the universe will respond to your efforts. The universe will always catch you if you have trust and allow the unfolding. You might fall faster than you anticipated or even bump something on the way that you will not understand or be able to identify, but ultimately all will be well when you are caught with your heart racing and every nerve ending on fire. This is the power and energy and magic of intention and change. This is living life to the fullest, our reason for being.

■ REIKI, NOT JUST A GARDEN TOOL ■

(OKAY, MY BROTHER WANTED ME TO CALL THE BOOK THAT, SO I HAD TO USE IT SOMEWHERE)

Why am I doing this and where does it all come from? you may ask. And I will tell you even if you didn't. I began actively exploring energy work about eight years ago, but really I must have been at it this whole time. Throughout my life I have sensed different energy in houses and places I have visited and have seen visions since I was ten years old—at least that is when I can remember seeing them, usually spirits or presences and whispers of past or future events. For years I mostly chose to absorb and internalize what I was sensing and feeling, but I finally allowed myself to be more open to the information. I was always curious but a little bit intimidated. I began acknowledging the energy shifts I would feel in myself in response to people and places and wanted to understand more about energy—how to use it to help me and others find clarity. My curiosity brought Reiki into my life. It is an ancient energy healing system with Japanese and Tibetan Buddhist roots. Much energy work, including Reiki, is focused on freeing trapped energy, or *chi*, and allowing it to flow through the body for wellness and balance. Freeing the energy implies new movement and inspired me to work with some clients on creating rituals for transitions in their life, to carry the movement into their physical and emotional worlds.

My visions became clearer as I learned and practiced Reiki and worked with energy in a more precisely focused way. Energy work is a reminder of what we already intuitively have the answers to. Freeing the energy brings the answers to the surface. The cells in our bodies hold joy and anger and all emotions and cannot lie. There is no escaping the truth when I work with clients on bringing that truth closer into their consciousness. My own intuitive voice has grown stronger and louder, and I am listening closely. I am continually and joyously struck by the raw power of the mind-body-spirit connection.

Being a visual person, I consciously use images in my work with clients, as well as receive them during sessions. I will never forget the first time I worked with a client undergoing radiation as a part of cancer treatment. She was suffering from burns as a result of the treatment. During the session, I visualized placing a cool blue healing ice pack on her burns as I worked. At the end of the session, she opened her eyes and smiled and said, "I feel so relaxed and it felt as though your hands were ice packs on my burns." I hadn't told her what I was visualizing during the treatment, but the power of tapping into universal energy is that remarkable, that accessible. When there are no blocks to the exchange of energy, it is absolutely effortless, like breathing. I don't suggest we take either for granted, but rather recognize it, use it, and appreciate it.

I have seen my clients access and understand the energy within and around them to heal and to find peace and new insight into their lives. I have worked with several enlightened surgeons on people and animals in operating rooms as a part of a wellness team with fascinating results—quicker and easier recovery times, minimum postoperative pain, and greater sense of ease going into the operation itself. One surgeon pointed out to me that a relaxed body was much easier to operate on than a tense body. Why all surgeons wouldn't want their patients to be relaxed and confident before surgery and to heal as quickly as possible is a mystery to me. I am more and more excited to hear of more hospitals and clinics offering Reiki and other energy work as part of their service options. Traditional and nontraditional healing methods can partner very well together.

Many of my Reiki clients are initiates to alternative energy work, but even the skeptical folks are surprised at the results of accessing energy they hadn't been aware of before. The physical repercussions of stress, spiritual and emotional disconnection, and splintered faith have lead them to search for a better understanding. They are beginning to integrate an awareness of the mind-body-spirit ties, but are looking for more. Traditional Western theories and textbooks have not provided the complete understanding or ease they seek. It has become more widely accepted to search elsewhere, and we are. We are looking to Buddhist, Native American, and pagan cultures for their spirit and nature-oriented traditions. And hopefully we arrive as students, receptive and respectful, not cultural carpetbaggers, appropriating customs and sacred ways without understanding or permission. That is a violation of universal trust. I will get down from my soapbox now.

We are going back to church and the communities they provide and looking for God or a flicker of the Divine in our daily lives. Something is missing and we may not be able to pinpoint it exactly, but many of us are willing now more than ever to explore and see what our spiritual adventures reveal.

What will be revealed will not always be easy to look at, acknowledge, or act upon. Some of you, I know, are looking for guidance in times of crisis, physical or spiritual, while others are looking for motivation for change or help with life passages. I can tell you that I've seen people undergo amazing transformation of spirit and strength through heightened self-awareness and a deep understanding of the energy that abounds within them and in the universe. This is how significant and lasting life changes are made. The journey never ends, for each new circumstance brings new decisions and choices to make. When we understand our role as maestro in the process is when we can revel in life and infuse our symphony with joy.

Each and every one of us holds tremendous power to heal ourselves and others, that I know to be true. Often my clients arrive with questions they may not be able to articulate yet. They just know that something is not quite right in their world—physically or energetically. They are willing to explore the possibilities, open doors to the unknown parts of their spirits and uncover the fear, pain, joy, and path to clarity that lies within. That is what I'm hoping will happen for you.

SEPARATION, AWARENESS, UNDERSTANDING

■□■□■□■□■□■□■□■□■□■□■□■□■□■□■□■□■□■□■

Gretel Ehrlich witnesses a Sun Dance, a most holy religious ceremony of the Plains Indian tribes:

All afternoon the men danced in the heat—two, eight, twenty of them at a time. In air so dry and with their juices squeezed out, the bouncing looked weightless, their bodies thin and brittle as shells. It wasn't the pain of the sacrifice they were making that counted but the emptiness to which they were surrendering themselves. It was an old ritual: separation, initiation, return. They'd left their jobs and families to dance. They were facing physical pain and psychological transformation. Surely, the sun seared away preoccupation and pettiness. They would return changed. Here, I was in the presence of a collective hero. I searched their faces and found no martyrs, no dramatists, no anti-heroes either. They seemed to pool their pain and offer it back to us, dancing not for our sins but to ignite our hearts.

■ □ ■

from *The Solace of Open Spaces*
— Gretel Ehrlich

SEPARATION

■□■□■□■□■□■□■□■□■□■□■□■□■□■□■□■□■

You may have to remove yourself from the noise of your everyday world in order to figure out where to begin. You cannot squeeze life in between working longer hours but less productively, driving the children all over creation, justifying staying home yet another Friday night, and watching the eleven o'clock news. When that becomes the pattern, you may wake up one day and say, "Damn, how did that happen?" or worse, "I can't believe I am so miserable. Clearly it must be someone's fault."

In order to accomplish this first step of getting back in the life adventure, you are going to have to commit to making your time and your life a priority. You may be battling your own fears as well as other people's to get this done. Try to avoid taking on anyone else's ANYTHING if you can, because that just makes the bag you will be left holding just a wee bit too heavy. No one likes it when someone else changes the routine or goes against the grain, because then we have to examine what might need fixing in our own lives. Everyone will try their hardest to reel you back to them or to where and how they know you. We all constantly try to put one another in context against our own canvases. Beware and be aware of it and also pay attention to when you judge others. We can throw a tremendous amount of energy at envy and jealousy. It will only ever result in lost opportunity to celebrate the successes of others and to mirror what we want in our own lives, and therefore deny ourselves our dreams.

■ DREAM DATE ■

The first time you make time for yourself will be the hardest, so make it next to impossible to find an excuse to get out of it. Better yet, before you go to sleep tonight, say into the night, "I would really like some time to myself without all the noise," and then drift off to sleep with happy fantasies of how you would spend that time. If you find yourself coming up with reasons why you can't do this, then you are not ready. It may feel overwhelming or you may not truly believe that you deserve this chance, but deserving has nothing to do with a life filled with joy. If you talk yourself out of it easily, then you are not ready to take this first step. If you are not ready to read and use the book, that is just fine, but know that and give yourself credit for getting to here. I am trying reverse psychology on you. Is it working? Maybe the book will sit on the shelf or by the bed for some time, but know that you have already initiated change. It may take several rounds before you make it all the way through. It may take several tries before you make it through the first section. Each time you go back you will have greater strength, but that is not all you need. You will need faith and trust to get on the solid ground. Sometimes it takes a windy, sideways route to find it, and therein lies adventure, if you choose to look at it that way.

Carefully plan your time away like a secret mission, down to the last detail if that makes it more likely that you will follow through with it, as long as you are clear that this is what you want. Do not muddy the water with questions of merit or feasibility, just whisper your desire into the universe. Travel undercover at first, too. You don't have to announce to everyone what your plans are, because then you will have thirty opinions (read: noise) that will start to wear you down. Congratulations, you have just initiated change, again. Could this get any simpler? The universe doesn't miss a trick—it knows what you want and is just waiting for you to get out of the way. Are we good at putting up roadblocks to our wildest dreams, or what? I think it is time to start taking them down.

■ GETTING OUT OF DODGE ■

The most challenging part of the journey may be this first step—to separate yourself from your everyday world in order to find the stillness to look at the truth of where you are beginning. You must physically and emotionally separate yourself from your everyday world to take the time to discover what you want to shift or how you want the energy to change within you or around you. This in itself is the most important action in the process of change. You are making the commitment by telling yourself (and ultimately the world) that this is your priority. All commitment triggers the flow of movement.

This is where we begin to change the selection of tapes playing in our heads—you know, the ones about what we deserve and why, who is preventing our happiness, why we are not worthy, how bad we look in those pants, the state of the economy, both global and personal, all the good ones are taken, etc. Yeesh, the noise we walk around with in our heads (and ultimately our hearts, stomachs, lungs, and every tiny cell). No wonder there is little room for joy in there. So, let's make some space.

Take a look at the energy within you, what you send out, what you hold on to, and what that means to who and where you are now. Ta-da—the truth, always the best place to begin. Energy shifts and the momentum of change begin with your thoughts, both conscious and unconscious. Your thoughts and emotions have tremendous power, and it is here where we begin to find clarity.

In order to make room for ideas and desires that may be lurking in the background, dying for a little airtime, you have to get out from underneath some of the noise. That means pulling yourself out of your everyday environment, where you are tugged at and expected of and taken over by others and by your own list of preoccupying thoughts. Women are particularly good at getting so wrapped up in everyone else's life—partner, friends, children, coworkers—that we don't have time to look at our own lives. Thank God, right? We might be quite alarmed to discover how we spend our energy each day and night. We'll get to that later on in the book, so don't think you're off the hook. You had better take a look, because that is your truth. Life at this moment may not be all that we had hoped or wanted, and that implies living with it or changing it—neither option is easy. Personally, I'd rather work on the possibility of attracting more joy than face the certainty of "more of the same."

▪ QUIET ON THE SET! ▪

If you decide to face the challenge and look under the surface, you are going to need the space and quiet to do it in. Internal noise appears in the form of fear, expectations, emotional scars, and guilt. External noise bombards us from ourselves, our lovers, friends, relatives, children, employees, bosses, the radio, television, gossip, traffic, and all those details—PIN numbers, cell phone numbers, access codes, etc. You don't stand a chance unless you get the hell outta Dodge and find a few moments of peace and quiet. Physically removing yourself from your environment is step one of breaking free from your emotional, physical, and spiritual routines. The more you do it, even for short periods, the easier it will become.

The separation and quiet brings clarity and strength in preparation for crossing the next threshold, which is to see where you are going. First, you have to see where you are now. Thought and contemplation is the first part of picking up on the rhythm of change. To accomplish this you will need to find someplace to retreat to. Change is a journey into the unknown, where you may have to come face-to-face with parts of your life that are painful. But change is necessary for us to move forward, to push through the hard parts, the fear. We all have fears that challenge us, and all those pieces and pictures and emotions that we do not want to face may keep us stuck in place. We may look away from fears and challenges, hoping they will go away or change on their own. They won't. They will stay the same or intensify, especially if we choose to ignore them or choose to let them run our lives by inviting them in to stay.

■ THE FEAR DOG—A BRIEF DISCUSSION ■

Our fears are unruly and messy, layered with memory and experience and oh-so-much emotion. Our fear-filled reality, although valid, is created in the past and then compounded daily if we let it. Change, risk taking, and movement happen in the present, but fears can become deeply rooted, difficult to access and understand at times, too. The idea is to understand them so that you can recognize when you are responding to a situation in fear. Recognize your fear triggers so that you can move through them. You don't want to stay in a place of fear. Who even wants to look at them, though? What a gruesome thought. Talk about scary. Fear is like the dog at the party that immediately jumps in the lap of the one person in the room who doesn't like animals. The fear dog will follow you around like you have pâté on your pants leg if you try to ignore him—pesky, persistent, and annoying. Don't try to shut fear out completely, because I promise you he won't go away. Pet him on the head to acknowledge him and then keep going. Walk away and don't look back. He'll be sitting right there where you leave him. Just put a little distance between you and him. Woof.

Many of our actions, non-actions, and reactions are in response to fear. Remember, the energy you put out is the energy you attract. You can't get very far on your journey if you are stuck in fear. What do you fear the most? What makes you lie awake at night, bite your nails down to the quick, or engage in destructive behavior patterns? As a matter of fact, don't answer that question, don't even think about it, because you will get stuck on that fear and all the emotions and disruption that go with it. Instead, think about something that makes you blissfully happy, something that makes you feel confident and strong. Ready? Think happy.

▪ SERPENTINE, SHEL ▪

Fear finds us in complacency and predictability. Bobbing and weaving through life, flowing with change makes it harder for fear to find you. Did you ever see the movie *The In-Laws* with Alan Arkin and Peter Falk? Go rent it even if you have seen it. I dare you not to laugh. So, the two men's kids are about to marry and the families will be joined. Alan Arkin plays Sheldon, a mild-mannered dentist, and Peter Falk is an undercover agent who drags Sheldon oh-so-reluctantly into his assignment. In one scene they are at an airport, on the runway, when suddenly they are being shot at. Alan Arkin starts running, but Peter Falk makes him go back and run in a serpentine pattern because he will be less likely to get hit, screaming at him, "Serpentine, Shel, serpentine!" Sounds like good advice to me.

If fear is the primary number in your equation of change, then it becomes the focus EVERY time you are faced with change of any kind, like getting stuck in the same tire rut in your driveway after the ground freezes. Doesn't it feel great when you bust out of it? The expression "living in fear" to me describes someone devoting all of his energy to feeding his fears. Fear will eat a lot of energy if you let it. Fear will eat so much energy, there will be nothing left for anything else. Fear will eat the energy meant for joy, the energy meant for hope, and the energy meant for love. There is no way to abolish all fear from our lives, nor should we.

A dash of fear can be motivating and an instigator for action and change. Fear may finally get us to change self-destructive behaviors we have continued leading our lives with. Sometimes, it has to get pretty bad before we are afraid, but it can force us to act. When our behavior or addictions have cost us relationships, jobs, and our health, fear may be constructive to help us save our own lives. That is reality-based fear. Emotion and memory-based fears are the ones that trip us up or keep us at a standstill. Take a look at how much fear you hold on to, how much energy you give it, and then make a long list of all that you want in your life, from emotions to things to situations. Move through and away from the fear to the place of possibility and desire. Okay, enough about the f-word.

■ OUR LIGHT ■

Understanding the energy in and around us asks us to listen to and trust our intuitive voices. Every time you ignore your intuitive voice, you will stumble. Sometimes, we intentionally ignore our intuitive voice because we see the message coming through as too challenging. Well, staying where you are and being miserable or less than you could be may be less challenging, but how does that contribute to your individual fulfillment or contribute to the world's energy landscape? In the grander scheme of existence and perpetuating life in the fullest sense, we all have an obligation to be our biggest selves.

Gandhi tells us that "we must be the change we wish to see." Living a full, happy life allows us to bring the world along for the ride. When we do allow our own lights to shine brightly, our joyous energy becomes contagious. It brings timid and reluctant souls out of hiding, perhaps making them more willing to take their own risks in pursuit of joy. This is the path to enlightenment.

Our light is the responsibility to hold close and act upon all of life's possibilities. Our power is a big, joyous, limitless obligation to follow the path that leads us to our being our highest selves, an active, intentional participant in universal exchange of energy.

■ RITES OF PASSAGE ■

In this culture we tend to avoid adversity and challenge at all costs, anything to numb ourselves and silence our fears. This is exactly when judgment and our critical voices grow louder. And we turn these voices against ourselves and others and ultimately block out the truth and any hint of all that is possible. Many cultures include rites of passage, spiritual journeys, or tests of inner strength as a part of the transition to adulthood or transition within society. Initiates are sent to walk into the fire that houses their innermost fears. They must ask for guidance and trust that they will be answered with a hint of the truth. They may not always receive the answer they want or expect but must have the courage to accept the response and have faith in themselves to carry out their tasks. This is what you are being asked to do by removing yourself from your daily life. It is the first stage of your rite of passage, making space for change to take hold.

■ YOUR TIME ■

Remember when you learned to tie your shoes or ride a bicycle or drive a car with a stick shift? At the time it may have seemed as if you would never get the hang of it, but now you can't remember not knowing how to do it; it has become a part of your inherent vocabulary. That is meaningful change and integration of a proficiency as a way of life, second nature, part of your skill set, part of you. It takes practice and it takes effort. The first step is to quiet the noise of your everyday world for a bit to look at where you are. You need to focus and turn down the volume of channels running in your head that are telling you to remember to pick up the dry cleaning, plan that party, finish that report, make a dentist appointment, pay bills, take the dog to the vet, and buy a birthday present for your nephew. Oh, and don't forget to lose fifteen pounds by your high school reunion, rediscover passion with your mate, become vice president of your company, and win the "parent of the year" award.

Allowing yourself to break away from your everyday life for a few hours or a day to begin to understand the changes you want in your life is a passage into the world of possibility. Give yourself this chance to access your true desires for a full life. Don't censor your thoughts or edit your emotions as they appear.

Reach inward to your true, authentic self and trust the guidance that awaits. Separate yourself physically and emotionally from where you are and push your consciousness beyond its everyday place; fantasize and explore your dreams. Therein lies the call and answer prayer for change.

■ STORY: BE WHERE YOU NEED TO BE ■

A woman I know joined an exercise class with several friends. It was a great idea at first. They knew that they would all see one another regularly and it would be fun to start out together. For the first month Pam loved the new routine. It turned into a social occasion, each of them catching up on their lives before and after class. One day Pam realized that she loved seeing her friends at class but that she was distracted. She found herself unable to get away from her thoughts about her own life or even those of her friends and focus on the physical routine, which she had come to love. They had purposefully chosen a class that was not very demanding. It had been kind of a lark at first, but Pam was becoming aware of her growing strength and desire to concentrate on testing herself physically. Pam wanted to focus on the physical exercise, and she joined another class. Her friends initially resisted and resented Pam's wanting to leave to join a more advanced class. At this point, Pam could have decided to stay in the easier class and make her friends happy, assuaging their fears about their own lives (wrong answer, but you knew that, right?). But instead, Pam moved onto the more challenging class. The group then decided to plan to all get together regularly once a month for dinner and supported their friend's courage to challenge herself. Pam didn't have to give up important time with her friends, but she could also push herself and focus on her relationship to her physical self. She made herself and her well-being the priority in her plan. Pam is feeling more confident about her body's strength and flexibility and feels that it is carrying over into her personal and work lives as well. She recently resolved a situation of misunderstanding with a coworker that had caused her anxiety for months. She initiated the conversation that cleared the air and made her work environment much more peaceful. Exercise has become Pam's meditation time, a way to clear away noise and appreciate the unfolding momentum of change in her body and spirit.

■ EXERCISE: JUST SAY NO ■
(TO NANCY REAGAN AND ANYONE ELSE WHO ASKS FOR A FAVOR)

This week you need to say no to one favor or a usual plan that takes up your time. It doesn't mean you have to scream at someone if he asks you for something (although you may feel like it) and you don't have to offer an explanation. "I'm sorry, I can't" is all you have to say; otherwise, you will be talked back into it, I guarantee you. Don't waffle.

Say yes to your happiness and take yourself somewhere alone—a coffee-house, dinner, drop-in yoga class, the park, somewhere that the usual suspects in your life won't be able to track you down and engage you. Go somewhere you don't know everyone also not your regular hangout—in other words, because you won't find quiet there. There is comfort in going to a place where people know you, but it can also be distracting.

In preparation, don't read the newspaper, listen to or watch the news for the day; instead, keep your energy focused on your inner world and even try to limit interactions with people. Line up that sitter now. Don't schedule meetings or appointments that day. If you are staying home, unplug the phone or at least turn it off so you won't be distracted by the ring. If you normally spend time exercising, then do a different activity that isn't competitive or goal-focused. Go for a walk—a long, slow one—and don't bring your cell phone, whatever you do. Kayak on the river. Drop by a salsa dance class. Find an inspirational quote or a poem that makes your whole body smile and carry it around in your pocket all day. Read it twenty-five times today.

Being alone with yourself may be very difficult, but it is really all right if your voice mail picks up the calls. In the silence is where the change process begins. This is your chance to focus on your self and your place in the world. It may sound too simple to just be in new or different surroundings, but it is unusual for many of us to experience it and it is powerful. A small shift in focus is the point. Use your journal, if you have one, or start one to make notes about any feelings or thoughts that come up. Don't write immediately, just be for a bit. It takes some time to quiet our minds. See how it feels and what thoughts occupy your mind. What is hidden underneath? Try to let go of all the thoughts crowding your head. Let them drift away. Silence with ourselves brings our focus to the present.

AWARENESS

■□■□■□■□■□■□■□■□■□■□■□■□■□■□■□■□■

Okay, so now you are officially in training to shift your focus and the thoughts that dominate your world. The next task involves actually noticing the world around you and then your place in it—how you crash around in it, ignore it, or tiptoe around in it. I am hoping that soon you will be dancing and singing and laughing through most of your days, or at least smiling more. Not superficially, either, but with your whole body. We will be practicing whole-body smiling all the way through. Notice the world around you and your place in it—every little thing can make you sing and dance and smile.

Making the time won't be as much of an issue with this step, but you will have to be willing to open your eyes, your mind, and your heart. If negative images and emotions hold a significant place in your life, then taking steps to becoming more aware of beauty and possibilities may be challenging for you. What are you most aware of in your world? Pain or splendor? Obstacle or possibility?

■ SMOOTH MOVE, GRACE ■

Living a life of awareness is actively participating with your eyes and ears and heart open. When you are aware, you are better able to see your role in the world—how you interact in it and with it. It will train you to notice energy shifts and clues or answers that may appear on your path. You become aware of your internal and external surroundings and the subtleties and the grandeur of space and place and time together. If you pause to see the world around you and discover the beauty in the ordinary and everyday, you will begin to navigate with your internal receptors turned on—looking from the inside out—from your heart and your soul. You will dramatically change your perspective. Beauty will be the familiar rather than the exception. There surely must be mystery and intrigue in the everyday, or we wouldn't smile when we pause to notice a vision as simple as a lone red umbrella against a gray sky, blue-white snow blanketing the branches of a pine tree, a delighted old couple holding hands, or a full moon rising up huge in the night sky.

Recognizing and acknowledging our external surroundings feeds our energetic selves. It restocks the energy pantries deep with in us and makes room for grace and possibility. Anne Lamott's version of grace is the one I am talking about:

Grace is the light or electricity or juice or breeze that takes you from that isolated place and puts you with others who are as startled and embarrassed and eventually grateful as you are to be there.

Getting to grace will mean stumbling and righting yourself along the path as you go. We are working toward feasting on the energy of an ease about giving and receiving love and joy from our surroundings, from one another and from ourselves. Try to take smaller bites of anger, resentment, and fear. Take huge, delicious bites of beauty, love, and kindness.

■ TWEAKING YOUR SENSES ■

Another way to connect to the earth, your self, your history, and the Divine is through the five senses. Aren't there certain smells that carry you to other places when you happen upon them again? I was walking down the street in New York not long ago and suddenly reeled around to find the origin of a smell. The spicy, burnt fragrance was layered and utterly unique, and smelling it again instantly sent me back to Madras in southern India. I had encountered it nowhere else, and to me that smell signifies the complex splendor of that country. Does the smell of baking bread make you sigh? And freshly cut grass; the raw, mineral smell of the ocean; fresh peaches; babies' skin; musty, dusty books; or your lover's pillow—where do these aromas send you? Our sensory recollections are very powerful; some memories don't easily fade. How thrilling to recall them and bring them flooding to the surface.

■ CHOOSE ANOTHER AROMA ■
(IF LAVENDER MAKES YOU GAG)

Discover what scents and sights and touches have significance for you. I include aromas and herbal extracts in my Reiki practice, as well as music, color, and light. Over time I have recognized which scents I respond to and how they affect me and have encouraged my clients to do the same. Many books have been written that discuss aromatherapy and herbal remedies. Some are very informative with guides for specific desired results and the properties of the different scents. But just because lavender is supposed to have a calming effect and induce general feelings of well-being doesn't mean it will for you if you can't stand the smell. A general olfactory aversion or a strong negative reaction often has to do with sensory memory.

We all have certain aromas that remind us of people or places and scents that transport us right back to a specific place. I happen to love lavender because it reminds me of my grandmother and the drawer in her bathroom filled with scented soaps. To a child, the drawer was magical. When we were visiting, I would sneak into the bathroom during naptime, open the drawer, and inhale the exotic flavors. Heaven. I adopted the habit later on and always have a "smelly soap drawer" wherever I live. I found out recently that my aunt has one, too. Now years later the vanity remains in my grandmother's house, and though she is gone, the drawer still smells like lavender and roses and cucumber and lemons all at the same time. She is in the room with me when I open that drawer, and I feel her peaceful presence.

■ EYE TWEAK ■

All that we witness with our senses gets stored in our imagination banks. We can draw upon any of it for strength and context and remembrance. Our souls may be "glimpsed once, imagined for a lifetime," offers Seamus Heaney, and sensory memories are the same way. Beauty provides us access to our souls. Acres of wild irises at the top of a mesa, acts of courage, a great blue heron taking flight, true love, the early evening sky? What visual experiences get caught in your throat? Have you seen people you have known and loved in the faces of strangers?

Diane Ackerman writes in *A Natural History of the Senses:*

It probably doesn't matter if, while trying to be modest and eager watchers of life's many spectacles, we sometimes look clumsy or get dirty or ask stupid questions or reveal our ignorance or say the wrong thing or light up with wonder like the children we all are.

It doesn't matter if you get dirty or look clumsy, but it does matter that you look. And it does matter what you see and how you see it.

■ WALKING WITH A GYPSY ■

I met a woman once in my old neighborhood in the city. I didn't meet her exactly; we just ran into each other a lot. We often ended up walking down the same street at the same time. We were both on our way to the greengrocer's or the Middle Eastern specialty shop, which were next door to each other. She told me she was a Gypsy. She was tiny with huge, fancy gold swirly eyeglasses, always a cigarette dangling from her lip and clutching a leopard-skin case. She walked as though she owned the street. I believed she did. She knew everyone and had something to say about each one as we passed by. She always greeted me as if we had known each other forever. As I fell into step with her, I entered the conversation midstream. It was always as if we had just been talking, got separated by a streetlamp, and met up again just on the other side, even if I hadn't seen her in days. She never asked my name, nor I hers. As we walked, every once in a while she would spit and say something to herself. One day I asked her why she did that. She said that whenever she saw something ugly she had to spit and say a prayer asking not to ever have to see anything as horrible again. Pretty soon we were both walking and spitting and mumbling when we met. I changed my route one day to avoid running into her. I didn't want to focus on the ugliness anymore. I wanted to make space in my mind and body for beautiful things, and I had gotten used to looking for the ugly in the neighborhood that I loved. This was just not working for me at all. The contradiction made me shift my focus. Sigh, then I had great fun walking around, remembering and discovering all that I found lovely in and around my favorite haunts. If you see, feel, hear, or taste something extraordinary, or especially ordinary, acknowledge it, whisper hello in appreciation. It isn't very difficult to find beauty in the world.

■ TOUCH TWEAK ■

Hot sand running through your fingers, a new someone's eyelashes brushing your cheek, rubbing your feet between new flannel sheets, freshly fallen snow under your boots, a bumpy turtle's back, a little one's hand in yours, the softest part of your dog's ears. I don't know about you, but I just about can't stand how soft my dog's ears are. I make her crazy by always wanting to touch them and hold on to them. She eventually gets annoyed but I am in heaven. What makes you tingle all the way to your core?

I was walking in the woods once when I came upon a pile of feathers. A ruffed grouse had fallen prey to a hawk or some other predator. I picked up a few of the brown and white streaked feathers and brushed them against my cheek, imagining the bird in flight. I put the feathers in a leather pouch I have on the rearview mirror in my car. Sometimes when I am sitting in traffic I reach out to touch them and am calm. Do you have touchstones or talismans that make you smile and remember or take you somewhere wonderful?

■ TASTE TWEAK ■

Why is it that certain foods you loathed with every ounce of your being as a small thing one day become palatable and sometimes even delicious? Our taste buds must mature along with the rest of us. Taste is a matter of taste after all. There may be many different versions of mashed potatoes, apple pie, or meatloaf, but all of us have memories of how we expect them to taste. Demand them to taste. Need them to taste. Tastes we know can ease our worries momentarily and remind us of being loved and bring experiences right into the open. Remembering the first time you tasted certain things can be powerful memories and stay with you always. There is always a story that goes with the first taste. The first snowflake every season, a kosher pickle from the deli, the first bite of grouper fish sandwich on vacation, anything wildly spicy followed by a sip of cold beer, carrots and tomatoes and raspberries and anything just picked from the garden, maple sugar candy poured right in the snow, salty french fries, of course. Those are just a few from my list. Now it is your turn. Discovery of new tastes and rediscovering favorites is a great adventure.

■ EAR TWEAK ■

My sister's dogs let out huge sighs when they lie down. We call them "happy collie noises." It makes me laugh every time. Hearing my nieces call my name, laughs from all the way down inside, anyone singing "Amazing Grace," especially Judy Collins, a flock of geese overhead in the autumn, the brook running behind the house, the coyotes talking to one another in the back field, and Jimi Hendrix's guitar playing—those are sounds that make me tingle. I have heard that mothers can pick out the voice of their child in a crowd of crying babies. What are the sounds that stir your soul or quicken your heart?

It is important to discover what excites your spirit. Ultimately it may not matter why you are attracted to certain scents or aromas, colors, textures, or sounds, it just matters that you are aware. It is part of your profile, what makes you, you.

■ A THING OF BEAUTY ■

One of my English teachers in high school would not allow us to use the word "thing" in any writing assignment. He believed that it was lazy writing. We were not allowed to resort to using a "catchall" word when given a bit more thought, we could most likely come up with a more descriptive phrase. I have never forgotten that and for years afterward "thing" took on a new meaning for me. In my freshly imprinted mind, the word "thing" suddenly implied only objects, concepts, or ideas that had no significance or were of no consequence. Later on I came to believe that whereas my teacher may have been right that there can be more creative uses of description, "things" still can be wondrous. Things in or out of their usual context can be extraordinary. Have you ever been walking down the street and had a paper cup follow you in the wind? As you walk, it rolls and bounces along with you? Suddenly the world is altered and shrinks down to just you and the cup tagging alongside you like a puppy. Something shifts in my universe when this happens. I feel as if I am onstage and have momentarily forgotten my lines. What happens next? Am I the one in control, or is some other force pulling the strings? It reminds me that I am in a relationship with each and every part of the universe, including the wind and paper cups—all things.

■ STORY: MORNING BREAKS ■

One of my daily morning rituals is to walk with my dog on the beach for an hour or so. I try to get there just before dawn so that I can be a part of the transition to the new day. It is my time for prayer and contemplation. I often meet others at the beach conducting their morning rituals: Andrea with handsome Jake, a Bernese mountain dog cross; Richard and the lovely Hannah, a happy, squirmy golden retriever; Anne with her noble rescued Siberian, Grania; Mike and Jaffy, the running boys; and Jane with Otis, her subdued older setter, and Rocky, a young mix. Rocky has the same colorings as Otis, but is a bag full of energy and grins and throws you his salesman's personality before you even get up close. We all passed one another on the beach several times before formally introducing ourselves. We would always greet each other the same way no matter what the weather, though: "Unbelievable day, isn't it?" "Extraordinary," the other usually answered. We do this every morning and I am challenged to find new and true words to describe my surroundings inside and out. I cherish my time alone by the sea, and people are respectful of others' desires for solitude or company. If my fellow beach travelers catch me in a moment when I have slipped away from the gratitude of the day, they bring me right back with "Isn't the sky beautiful right now, just this minute?" We are all awe-inspired at every turn. The beach is always surprising, in flux. Sometimes it is violent, sometimes soft and gentle . . . clouds that skim by in so many incarnations, driftwood that appears from the sea like mythical creatures crawling up to the shore, and colors in the sand or water that make you sigh as you try to file them away in your memory.

In *An Unspoken Hunger*, Terry Tempest Williams describes her response to beauty:

I have felt the pain that arises from a recognition of beauty, pain we hold when we remember what we are connected to and the delicacy of our relations.

The first early-winter morning I arrived at the sea, a frost covered the landscape and I felt as if I were stepping out onto the surface of the moon. I wasn't sure if I was connected to the earth at all until I took the first step. Each new day I drink in the transformation from darkness to far-off color— from just a slice of sun to light changing so quickly, it almost seems to be pulsing in a stop-camera series of movements. My newly hatching world can change from a sky full of smudged purple balls of yarn to a raw, roasted red horizon and then to gray and white feather dustings of color against brilliant blue in a brief hint of a moment. If I turn away to look down at the sand and back again to the sky, I have been transported to some other beach, far away.

I was lugging a hunk of driftwood down the beach the first time Jane and I greeted each other. The piece of wood was long and craggy and looked like a miniature tree. I left my footprints and a long snaky trail in the sand behind me as I made my way along. We smiled as we passed each other, and Jane said, "Good morning. What an impressive piece of wood." I grinned and replied, "It is, a sculpture in its own right, don't you think?" "Indeed," she said, and smiled. "And what an extraordinary day."

This morning ritual gives me perspective each day on what is true and begins with simple gratitude for the wonder of the world I live in and the simple hearty connections with those out journeying, too. A woman I know once said, "If you do not have time to give thanks every day, how can you have time to live?" Living in awareness and gratitude is an active, conscious act, not something to pay lip service to and go through the motions with.

Beauty is not about just about fine art—paintings and sculptures and other representations and interpretations. Beauty lies within our connections and longings and in our everyday world and all we encounter. Today when I was walking near the marsh, I think I saw a duck for the very first time, really saw it. I had never stopped to notice the exquisite green color of a mallard duck's head. It is the richest, most regal color green I have ever seen. How did it get there? How could I have not noticed before? Today I saw a duck for the first time, really saw it. What are you seeing for the first time today? I invite you to discover and cherish the significance of "things."

■ EXERCISE: TEN BEAUTIFUL THINGS ■

Create a daily ritual of finding and acknowledging ten beautiful images on your way to work, or driving the children to and from school, or when you are out and about in the world. Expand your definition of beauty to include textures and contrasts, gestures, movement, and sound. Make a big space for beauty in your life. This exercise is designed for you to understand and subtly shift your energy focus in the world to the beauty and splendor all around you. And to lead you to a better understanding of what your focus has been up to this point. It is as simple as shifting your gaze ever so slightly in any direction. Now see what you have let into your world.

Involve your children, get it in their consciousness, too, to look, really look, at the world around them. Beauty is everywhere, in a simple gesture between two people, a hand reaching out to steady someone; the laughter of a stranger that reminds you of one that you love; a tree, big and solitary, standing its ground in the urban landscape; two birds singing back and forth on a wire; the glorious wrinkled hands of the man in the check out line in front of you; the smile on the face of the woman in the red car you let go ahead of you in traffic.

Do this every morning. Make it a morning ritual. Either say it out loud or write it in your journal, but it is important to somehow acknowledge what you are a witness to.

I know the path: It is straight and narrow.
It is like the edge of a sword.
I rejoice to walk on it. I weep when I slip.
God's word is: "He who strives never perishes."
I have implicit faith in that promise.
Though, therefore, from my weakness
I fail a thousand times, I shall not lose faith.

■ □ ■

from *All Men Are Brothers*
— M. K. Gandhi

UNDERSTANDING

How are you out there in the world? How do you interact? Does it match up with how you are on the inside? So, is it working for you? Yes? Then carry on. No? Well, then read on and we'll see what we can do.

You might need a bit of courage to look at the energy you give off and put out into the world. It may be revealing and it may be difficult. You will have to be fiercely honest with yourself in order to understand the energy you offer into the world. You may begin recognizing patterns of behavior or find yourself in similar situations over and over. It doesn't happen by accident. Look at your role in the scenes. You may still be holding on to someone energetically, even if he isn't in your immediate everyday life. That will keep you from moving on, and it may help attract similar people into your life now. It may be easier to let go or minimize the repeats if you can really see it. Often we are carrying it without even realizing that we are.

■ PERSONAL ALCHEMY ■

Our individual vibration in the universe is significant. Let's get fancy: it is our contribution to the collective energy landscape—our personal alchemy— how we recycle incoming energy and spin it back out into gold. The energy we bring into each room we enter, connections we make, and dreams we allow are the revelation of our true selves. It is our true dynamism, the beauty, pain, love, and fear we give off fused with what we let back in. Personal alchemy is what we hold on to that defines us organically. The energy we house can nurture us and others, support change, or drag us down like lead sinkers. Personal alchemy builds from discovery and acceptance of yourself at your highest spiritual level.

Discovering your inner gold can be a profoundly spiritual adventure. It involves listening to your intuition and understanding your true desires. Your intuition is in part energy messages that come in response to what you are putting out. You may fight or ignore your intuition every day. Often in hindsight you might say, "There was something about him or her that just didn't feel right," or, "I just had a funny feeling about the situation. I wish I had listened to my intuition." Listening to your intuition is a significant part of change. Your intuition is the truth. You have to trust yourself to make good decisions and you have to trust your intuition to help guide you. How many times have you been burned by not listening to your intuitive voice? You may follow your intuition at times without being fully conscious that you are doing it. You may sense an energy when you walk into a place and may not want to stay. Or you may feel adamant about defending a decision that goes against the general consensus, just because you have a clear feeling you are right. If you are aware and open, you will respond. When you are conscious and open to it, intuition can be very powerful. A friend of mine's true faith is based wholly upon her intuition. She has faith that her intuition will guide her to make the right decision, no matter how painful or challenging. She knows that when she does not listen, it can be even more distressing. Our intuitive voices may get drowned out by our analytical minds and rational thinking patterns. Intuition is like the tiny voices of the Whos down in Whoville, screaming to be acknowledged, that Horton the elephant finally heard. So, before you boil that dust speck and lose the opportunity to uncover a treasure chest of insight, listen a little bit more closely. Something's trying to get your attention.

■ BALANCING LIFE ■

A life in balance does not mean peace and quiet with all areas of your life humming along same old, same old. Balance is precarious, but in a big, exciting way. A life out of balance is spending your existence dwelling in only one domain, physical or emotional or spiritual. Each area needs attention and airtime. The balance comes in when you figure out which area you may feel strongest in at any given time and which areas could benefit from some of that strength. In my Reiki practice, I have worked with a number of athletes who are remarkably out of touch with their bodies in connection with their spirits and their emotions. They can push their bodies to extraordinary limits but may injure themselves repeatedly and look for a physical root to the problem, when it is likely to be found elsewhere. Many are not satisfied with their accomplishments and try to push themselves harder physically, without paying attention to any emotional roadblocks that may have been set up long ago. And also a remarkable number seem to substitute the extreme physical challenges for deep emotional intimacy.

For some it is easier to challenge themselves physically than to face emotional scars and confrontations. Developing a strong physical self takes tremendous discipline, as does developing a strong, brave spirit. There may be one area that you are stronger in than in others. That will likely shift throughout the course of each year, or even month. True balance is the knowledge that we can handle whatever comes up in life. We can ride out the tippiness. The dreams we wish to make real can come true, with the help of emotional, physical, and spiritual stamina.

■ ANIMAL INTUITION ■

Humans have the intuitive capabilities of other animals, we just often block it out with noise. Again, the noise is most often our fear. Animals are intuitive as a necessity for survival. They have two major puzzles to figure out during the course of a day and night: is it food, or could it kill and eat me? They have to read signs and give off signals to those they encounter. Animals don't have the filters, emotional barriers, and prejudices that we do. It is a very straightforward life. We can learn so much from them. I know I have.

When I do energy work with animals, it is never murky or ambiguous—they are all instinct. And they seem to have no fear of death. It is an accepted part of the cycle of life and their time on this plane. Their focus is indeed on survival and their role in the cycle, but it is based on pure innate knowledge. And because we have brought some animals into our world, they have to figure out how they fit into this society and pecking order. They never shut down their intuition.

Inka, one of my sister's collies, was having a malignant tumor removed from her jaw and I went into the operating room with her to do Reiki during her surgery. Before the operation, Inka and I were in the surgical prep area. I sat on the floor with her, waiting for the technicians to shave her and begin the anesthesia process. Inka had always loved having Reiki and was very responsive that day. I had known her since my sister first brought her home six years before. Now she was a new mom to seven beautiful puppies. This was a tough time for everyone. Inka was quite sick and tired from the recent whelp, and the cancer had appeared out of nowhere, it seemed. My sister was devastated by the diagnosis, and I wanted to do anything I could to offer support. Inka was normally quite the diva, barking at you and flipping your hand with her nose, demanding attention. That day she was quite subdued. She sat down right in my lap and stayed there until we had to put her on the table.

Collies are herding dogs; they must stay alert and always be aware of their surroundings in relation to the flock. To herd is their raison d'être, their true purpose. Any energy shifts must be evaluated as either a threat or a change of movement. Inka fought the anesthesia and tried her hardest to stay awake. It went against her core instinct to stay alert. To sleep on duty would mean certain failure. Her flock's as well as her own survival would be jeopardized. These instincts have not been bred out of these dogs even after years and years. The operation was a success, although surgeon Julie Bennett was frustrated not to be able to remove all of the tumor. She and other doctors were very pleased (and quite surprised) to see Inka wake up easily and be able to eat so soon after the radical surgery.

Surgery was followed by grueling radiation treatments. Midway through the series, my sister decided Inka had been through enough and brought her home. We make choices for the animals we have domesticated. Look into their eyes and they will tell you everything there is to know. It is our responsibility to monitor their quality of life and make decisions based on that visible and intuitive information rather than on our own selfish desires to keep them with us. Inka was ever the trouper throughout all the procedures, but my sister listened to her own intuitive voice telling her to stop. We were all hopeful that she would have more time, but one day a few weeks later my sister called me and said, "Inka's getting ready to die." She was sure. Liz and her dogs are very connected and she would have listening to her inner voice and watching signals from Inka. Liz brought her to Julie just to confirm what she already knew and then brought her back and settled her in on her favorite bed. Inka did die that night, at home and well loved. It was the best it could be. Liz trusted her intuition and followed through in faith. Loss is never easy, but we make the best choices when we let our own guard down, stay in the present, and allow the answers to come.

■ SPIRITUAL FITNESS ■

Taking care of your spiritual self is as important as taking care of your physical self.

Just as some of us postpone or neglect attention to our physical selves, many of us also neglect taking care of our spiritual selves. Spiritual fitness gives us strength to deal with challenges and adversity. Americans spend billions of dollars on their bodies—shaping them, trimming them, reducing them, and sculpting them by diet, exercise, and plastic surgery. What about spiritual fitness? How much time is given to taking care of the inside, our souls, our spirits? Your soul has to be thriving and be well fed and nurtured if your physical health is going to be at its peak. Our physical and spiritual selves cannot be separated—the wellness of both is essential. If you are willing to devote time and commitment to your physical body, what happens when you add your spirit? This is working toward wellness in the truest sense of the word. It is working toward a life in balance.

Our culture has become one of disorders and labels for every form of ennui and moodiness imaginable. There are depressive disorders, anxiety disorders, nutrition disorders, mood disorders, sleep disorders, impulse-control disorders, and seasonal affective disorder, to name just a few I've discovered. It may be easier to put a name tag on our feelings of confusion and longing for what we do not know and hide behind the diagnosis, but I would rather focus on living in wellness and possibility and joy. Building a protective wall behind these labels can provide a disservice, a place that promotes inertia or excuses for bad behavior. Delving into spiritual malaise is tricky and challenging, there is no doubt. Pain is real. Instead of immediately looking for "the answers," the antidote to make the pain go away, it makes more sense to understand what wellness and joy look like in our lives and tackle solutions from that angle.

■ It Is All in the Rhythm ■

Are you clear about the energy you put into the world and what you ask for in return? Understanding who you are puts you in place to know where you are in time as you begin to move with the rhythm of change. It makes me think of double Dutch jump roping. There are two ropes swinging and you have to figure out when and where to jump in so that you don't get caught in the ropes and break the rhythm. Where and how quickly you jump in may not be at all where you thought it would be. And it may not be when you think, either. The first couple of times you may get tangled up, but pretty soon if you start moving to the rhythm, you will be effortlessly in sync. It is all about rhythm—thrilling, joyous rhythm. Some days will be easier than others, and that is why working toward a life in balance is a source of strength.

Working toward balance and building skills to better handle the times when the scales are tipped and wobbly or when chaos suggests an appearance around the corner, is challenging but rewarding. Remember to look for the light when you are feeling as though you are sitting in the darkness. Look at any imbalances in how you expend your energy.

Where are you? Over here. And where is it that you want to be? Over there. So what are you doing still running in place over here? Shift focus. Change the rhythm. Let's dance.

■ STORY: BLACK-TIE BOWLING ■

The best party I ever went to was a black-tie bowling party years ago. Everyone invited was sent an extensive questionnaire as to our likes and dislikes that had to be returned before the party. Some of the questions were straightforward, and others were more obscure. We were encouraged to be creative with our answers, and prizes were offered as incentives.

The organizers could not have been more enthusiastic or welcoming when we arrived. Immediately, a high-energy tone greeted us when we walked in. One of the questions we were asked was what nickname we had always wished we had been given, and name tags with our choices were waiting for us. We were told that was to be our persona for the evening, and only at the end could we tell others our real names. We were split into teams, and people who knew one another were not allowed on the same team. We introduced ourselves to our team members, using our nicknames and in character. The rules for acquiring points for the team were very complicated. Most of the rules had little to do with bowling. Prizes were dangled in front of us for team spirit and cheerleading, among other things. They even hired as the judges foreign students who pretended not to speak English. Teams were penalized if members were caught trying to bribe the judges, but at the same time you were encouraged to try to get away with it. It was a raucous and hysterical atmosphere in our gowns, tuxedos, and bowling shoes. One woman on my team had gone to a salon to have her hair crafted into a beehive. She even wore a real bowling shirt over her dress, with a name stitched on the pocket. People were wildly creative and reveled in the freedom to pretend for one night. After bowling, we were ushered into a Chinese restaurant for the awards banquet. Not surprisingly, every team got an award.

This party was the great equalizer with made-up names, no chance for the "who are you and what do you do?" pressure until after we had been thrown together and worked as a team. None of that mattered. We were all in it together, connected by the game. We were in on the secrets. We could use our team and nicknames as an excuse to be freer than we may have normally been in a room full of strangers. We were also participating in a sport that most people are usually at about the same level. No one had to feel terrible for bringing the team down. We left feeling connected and hopeful, eager for similar experiences. We were encouraged to let go, be loud and creative. The energy at the party throughout the whole evening was full and joyous, close to bursting. I think I screamed a little louder and cheered a little more enthusiastically than I might have meeting people for the first time under other circumstances. It was safe to reveal more of the me, take the risk. The truth does in deed set you free, if you only let it.

■ EXERCISE: ENERGY PIE CHART ■
(NOT AS DRY AS IT SOUNDS)

Do an energy-expenditure assessment on yourself, similar to a physical analysis before starting a workout or training program. Sit down and figure out how you spend your energy. Are you all externally focused, or internally? Does your primary energy feed fear and doubt, or joy and wonder? Do you worry what others might think? What are your strong areas and what are your weak spots? In other words, where are you leaking energy? What behaviors are you hanging on to that do not serve you any longer? What areas of your life do you give the most emotional energy to? What does it look like? Do you dwell in the emotional, physical, spiritual, or intellectual? Create a pie chart to help you visualize the process. What percentage of your energy is focused on anger, directed at yourself or others? What percentage is taken up with clear intentions and clear paths? What about your dreams and desires? Fill in the chart and take a look at it. Be truthful with your answers, as hard as that may be. What areas would you like to change? What needs to move in order to make room for new energy?

INTENTION, TRUTH, ACCEPTANCE

The great affair, the love affair with life, is to live as variously as possible, to groom one's curiosity like a high-spirited thoroughbred, climb aboard, and gallop over the thick sun-struck hills every day.

■ □ ■

from *A Natural History of the Senses*
— Diane Ackerman

INTENTION

The power of change is in the now, this very minute. It is as simple as shifting your gaze several inches to the left or right when you are standing anywhere. A whole new world opens up to you. Your intention for change is good to explore. What is motivating your desire for making your life or some aspect of it different? Finding clarity may be a challenge when exploring your intentions. It is important to know where you want to go but also to know where you are beginning from. What really needs to change, vs. what you want to change? Consider the journey as the most important part of the process. Are you making external or internal changes, or both? Who are you doing this for? Is anyone else involved with the intention? Is revenge, spite, or fear motivating any of your desires? I don't mean to put you on the spot like this, but it is good to know the truth and what you might have to wade through to get to the road. You don't have to necessarily banish those feelings immediately, just be clear if and how they are involved. What emotions are attached to your intentions? You won't be asking yourself these questions just once. It is part of the change process each and every time. Once you get used to asking the questions, it will become easier to answer them with clarity and confidence. Once you make any change, big or small, you will have a whole new set of decisions to make. This is the journey, finding your life's rhythm. When you get to a place of understanding, you will never look at the world the same way again. Now you will be seeing it as a vast horizon of possibility, pausing to focus not on any hurdles or roadblocks, but on the wonder and joy of moving toward your true desires.

CAN YOU EVEN DYE
■ MY EYES TO MATCH MY GOWN? ■

Dorothy asks that question in *The Wizard of Oz* when she and her traveling companions have finally arrived in the Emerald City and are getting makeovers. That line always bothered my sister when we were young. The idea of dyeing one's eyes was pretty terrifying to her. When you are young you can't imagine doing something so drastic to a part of your body, and for what purpose? But isn't that what we tend to focus on as we grow a bit older, making physical alterations? The buffing and fluffing distracted Dorothy and pals and made them feel good for a while, but it didn't necessarily get them home or help them find their heart's desires. If you change your eye color, cut your hair, buy new clothes, or have liposuction, you will indeed transform the external. I am not knocking a good dose of fluffing and pampering now and again, but it is wise to take it a few steps further. Transformation on the inside will be incomplete unless you do—same contents, just a spiffier package. External alterations may indeed trigger the momentum for internal shifts if we are aware and follow through with what we begin with clear intentions. We can keep changing the window dressing, but if we don't change the interior, it won't be true change, just the illusion of change. Initially, the only internal changes will be your perception of the external.

Internal change is the powerful integration of energy shifts from your physical, spiritual, and emotional realms. It helps to have clarity as to where you are trying to go and why. It is important to know if you are making plans because of others in your life, outside expectations, or truly because you see the journey as an adventure of discovery and living in rhythm. The clarity of our intentions comes from the awareness and discoveries of truths we have been building to this point. When we feed our spirits and bodies with courage and joy, we can achieve anything. When we leak energy to unproductive destinations, we are draining our spirits. With low spiritual energy there may not be much that seems possible. Clear intentions lead us to a place (ruby slippers: click, click, click) like home, our true selves.

Home in our hearts, minds, and bodies is our place of passion and knowledge. You will be able to feel the energy shift simply by aiming for the truth. An understanding and acceptance of the truth is liberating, too. You have cleared away the smoke and mirrors that you may have had in place for a lifetime and are able to see your place at this moment clearly. You may find yourself feeling stronger, more centered, better able to deal with challenging people or situations. This thoughtful action makes room for joy, adventure, and discovery. The way to make room is to change the focus from the anger, the resentment, and the fear that hold us in states of inertia, and shift to our true desires and a path toward them. There is no way to get anywhere with emotional roadblocks set up at every turn. Begin the process of change at a place of understanding and acceptance—true wisdom. In shifting our energy away from destructive behavior patterns, anger, and fear, and toward true joy, we are encouraged to be our biggest, most beautiful selves.

■ ANY STRINGS ATTACHED? ■

In other words: hands off the control button. A wonderful part of this journey is the surprises along the way. If we are too busy trying to control every outcome and everyone's reaction to all that we do and say, we will be very tired, frustrated, and likely to miss the sea of possibilities in every situation that appears. Change may involve reinventing yourself from the inside out, and who you are as you interact with, and in, the world. We need to explore where we are now and where we want to be. Sometimes it may seem easier to stay in bad relationships, jump into others right away, or remain at jobs that don't challenge us, because the familiar is a known entity. We know what we are up against and what our role is, even if it makes us unhappy. We have to look at these patterns and understand them in order to do something differ-ent the next time. The only behavior and beliefs we can change are ours. Give up trying to change other people's. It is just a big lesson in frustration. If you enter into a familiar situation with clear intentions of making the outcome different than usual, the only reactions you can control are yours. The others involved will then be forced to respond differently. Most often we set up blocks ourselves that we may not be aware are impacting us. When we are aware of where our minds and spirits stay focused, and we shift our energy to the possible rather than the impossible, all that we want will be yielded to us.

A client of mine is interested in getting pregnant, and it hasn't happened as easily as she had hoped. From the outset she has been very conscientious about taking care of her physical self and is also aware that her spiritual and emotional selves need to be at peace with this plan as well. She now focuses on visualizing making a safe, happy environment for the baby to grow inside and after it is born, rather than on the idea that she is not getting pregnant. She has such great insight into her own self that she did not try to get pregnant during a busy, stressful month at work. She also revealed that she was not excited about having the baby be born under a particular astrological sign, so she took a break for a while. She had set that outcome up in her mind; therefore, the universe couldn't possibly contradict that block. She is even more confident now that she will indeed get pregnant and has surrendered more of the control to the universe. There is no way she can be denied her desire if she stays on that track with her true feelings and trusts that it will all unfold exactly the way it is supposed to—perfect timing, perfect circumstances.

You are creating the change and the shift simply by your intention and the follow-through of the energy you put out, or hold on to, accompanied by your actions. This is the power and grace of clear intentions and being in true sync with your emotional self.

■ OPEN MIND, OPEN HEART ■

Living a life of awareness and intention has many layers. Awareness of your external as well as internal surroundings is one piece. Living with awareness of and responsibility for your intentions and actions is another. In our search for self and connection, it is natural to investigate other ways; in fact, it is essential. By experiencing alternative perspectives and practices, we discover our selves, our sources of strength and truth. A gentle reminder, however—we are obligated to approach all traditions and ways of life with humility and an open and humble heart. With courage we can take the steps toward meaningful change and make room for joy, creativity, and love. If we are willing to key in to the energy in and around the universe, to live in awareness and gratitude, we are afforded more glimmers into the mysteries and possibilities of life.

■ STORY: AN INTENTIONAL MOVE ■

Marie's intention was to move and take some time for herself to figure out the next chapter in her life. Marie knew intuitively she was making changes that would be difficult but had to be made for her to survive and ultimately journey toward happiness and fulfillment. She took the courageous step of quitting a longtime, well-paying, challenging job that no longer stimulated or fulfilled her. Marie had also become physically ill and in the midst of brave change held tightly to her faith in her decision. Marie realized that this move was dramatic but necessary. She was going to save her own life. She decided to rent out her condominium in the city and move down south, where she had family. The plan was to take some time in a new place to do some healing and thinking about what she wanted to move toward. She was making big, security-rattling changes. She was leaving familiar situations and emotions behind and heading off into the unknown. She needed to let go of the destructive emotions and motivations that had kept her trapped for some time and move with confidence toward her new life and new behavior patterns.

On a physical note, Marie had also developed nodules on her thyroid (fifth chakra—our voice, our will, our faith). At this point, she realized that she was the only one able to create her own path or to realize her dreams, and she had to do what felt right. She chose to have an operation to remove the nodules because the threat of cancer, although statistically quite low, was for her very real and very terrifying. The thyroid gland, a hormonal and metabolism regulator, is located in the neck right next to the parathyroid gland and the vocal cords. As with any surgery in a tight, compacted area, there was a chance of nicking the organs and glands nearby. Unfortunately some bruising took place during Marie's surgery, and as a result her calcium levels fell dramatically. She lost her voice, and the hoarseness was showing little signs of improvement. There was no evidence of cancer, and relieved, Marie did not immediately regret her decision to have the operation. Her doctors promised that the other problems would be fixed, and she chose to live with the results for a while.

Marie had made the life-change decision to move on, and now she needed a positive send-off, an affirmation that her choices, although frightening, were clear. We got together several weeks after the surgery. Her voice was still a hoarse whisper and she was losing confidence in her doctors' explanations at that point. She needed to feel more certain that she was solidly on her healing path.

Marie came to see me, on her birthday no less, and we bought candles. I asked her to choose two different colors, one she was not drawn to or could leave behind in the store and another she loved and wanted to have around her. She then made two lists, one of all the emotions and situations that she wanted to leave behind and let go of, and the other of all the possibilities that awaited her. She needed to ask herself what it was that she wanted to make room for and what she needed and wanted to let go of that was crowding her head and heart and stifling her voice. She worked on the lists one at a time and got more and more excited as she wrote. She burned each list in its respective candle, and Marie said good-bye and hello at the same time. The tears she wept were a great release, and laughter soon followed. She left feeling hopeful. When she got home that night, a friend of hers called to see how she was doing, and halfway through the conversation her voice came back.

She keeps the candles for her new life out and visible and put away the candles representing all she was letting go. She can always pull them out if she needs to let go of more or as a reminder of how far she has come. Marie has just settled into an apartment down south and has several new job offers. She is excited and hopeful about her new life and has a profound awareness of the mind-body-spirit connection.

■ EXERCISE: MAPS OF DESIRE ■

Committing your hopes, dreams, and desires to paper is very powerful and can uncover clarity that may surprise you. Playing with paper and glue and scissors is therapeutic and helps you tap into your unconscious mind, where all the good stuff lives. These treasure maps are a visual picture of your path to your life's wishes. It becomes recorded energy, a physical representation of your desires. By making a vivid illustration of the path you want, you have given energy to those ideas and breathed life into them to help them start to grow.

Set yourself up at a table with magazines, scissors, wrapping paper, old calendars, markers, paint, glue, and oversized blank paper. Don't panic about the arts and crafts aspect of the task. The goal isn't concerned with what it looks like but what it says, what we uncover from your dream world. Where do you want your path to go? What might you want to see and do along the way? What are you journeying toward? This is a thoughtful process, so jump in when you are ready.

Quiet your mind and start going through the magazines, pulling out all the images, textures, words, and colors that appeal to you. Don't ask why you tear or cut something out, just keep going and don't censor yourself. Take whatever draws you. You may be very surprised at what you create, but listen to your intuitive self when you are working on the project. Gather the images and textures and colors for a while and then have a look at what you have collected. You can then start laying images on the big piece of paper to see how it is working. Create a time line of five years or ten years from now, or just conjure up a new notion of change. What is it going to take to get to the treasure, and what is the treasure? What happens in between? Who or what is involved in the journey? This is your creative vision of change. Keep the map somewhere that you will see it at some point during your day. Let it flow. Don't overthink any of the process. Be open to creativity and your emerging truth.

TRUTH

You need to begin any process of change from a place of truth. Clear the path in order to head off in the direction of your desired end result, but move toward it from where you are now. And don't forget to sign up for the optional side trips along the way, for they can be most fun and enlightening.

The truth is the beginning point of any change, but it is not always easy to see what is there. We may not like what we uncover and have to admit to. It may be tempting to rewrite our story, invent a whole new reality even, but the value of the truth is in the present and not the past. The past has led you to this moment, to the beginning. It is what it is, there is no getting around that. You can wish it were different, but that doesn't alter it. You are the only one who can change what happens next.

■ TRUTH OR CONSEQUENCES ■

There are no right answers. In a world of no right answers, though, the only answer is the truth. Your truth right at this very moment is where you need to start if you are going to journey inward to reveal your authentic self and create meaningful change in your life. Getting inside to our very centers is looking at the pain and joy that reside there. We must look at it and feel it in order to understand and move through it. Getting beyond it is essential. Don't stay in that quicksand trap of the past; rather, recognize it and then step into the light of the truth of the present. It is not your truth from six years ago, because we are always changing, and not the truth as you would like it to be tomorrow. The emotional pieces from six or even twenty years ago are likely to be hanging on and taking up space, so it is good to see what is there. I have to say it again, though: there is no room in your physical, spiritual, or emotional realms for all of that noise from the past, so shake it off like a wet dog and make a beeline for the starting line, right here and right now.

■ YOU CAN OWN YOUR TRUTH . . . NO MONEY DOWN! ■

Your truth is this very moment, the you that you are. The truth is not the more compassionate you, not the twenty-pounds-thinner you, not the "really, I swear I am not a raving stress case" you, but the magnificently powerful you of today. The you that has hopes and dreams and desires just dying to come true. The you that is brave enough to see and respond to what is really there. Your truth is yours alone. It does not belong to anyone else. It is not your father's or your mother's or your seventh-grade science teacher's. It is not the one you have been told you should be or should have been. It is the complex and curious soul yearning to peek out and test its wings. You are sole owner of your truth, so why not have a look?

We have all done one or all of the following:

- lied to our: parents, teachers, therapists, lovers, best friends (but only because we really, really had to), priests, ministers, rabbis, and selves
- cheated on: tests, diets, partners, taxes, surveys, questionnaires, and ourselves
- dated/married wrong, stayed too long in destructive relationships, or run from ones that might have had a chance of being great
- said hurtful words deliberately
- become addicted to drugs, alcohol, food, power, bad relationships, or other dangerous behavior
- harbored ill will toward: the prettiest, handsomest, richest, or thinnest
- "borrowed" items from the workplace and/or the marketplace
- coveted other people's: husbands, wives, partners, or lives
- made promises we did not intend to keep
- felt compelled to acquire lots more, bigger, better, expensive stuff
- discovered a morbid fascination with other people's misfortunes

So, no wonder we have had no chance at making changes in our own lives, but let's move on. This book—and most important, life—is not about creating saints or having all perfect days. You will slip and crash around regularly and continually. Beginning from a place of truth and acceptance allows our strength in times of struggle to kick in that much faster. The goal is to make some room in there for joy so that it becomes the first thought you go for. Squeeze by the "what if . . . ," the "I'll never be able . . . ," and the "but I am supposed to be . . . " Put those all up in the attic with the rowing machine, ab cruncher, and computer boxes, or better yet, put them all out on the curb on trash day and get on with it.

So, now we have thrown open those attic doors and revealed ourselves, naked in our emperor's new clothes. We discover we are flawed just like everybody else. This is not the place for absolution from wicked acts, it is the chance to forgive our imperfections as humans and get on with it—to accept who we are now at this moment. And to forgive others in our lives for being imperfect as well and leave them be. Forgiveness is an action word that grows completely from our hearts, not just our minds. Spend the energy and then keep moving on your own voyage. The truth and active forgiveness are alive in the present, and that is where we need to start from. Remember, we are making room for what we discover we want most in our lives. That is what all of this is about.

Carl Jung phrased this thought beautifully when he wrote:

Nowhere are we closer to the sublime secret of origination than in the recognition of our own selves, whom we always think we know already. Yet we know the immensities of space better than we know our own depths, where even though we do not understand, we can listen directly to the throb of creation itself.

Creation is the profound and wondrous result of change born from a place of truth and trust and believing all things are possible.

■ AND YOU WOULD BE? ■

In college I asked my friend if he were to die tomorrow, how would he want to be remembered? He said he wanted people to say he was sexy (it was the early '80s, give him a break). He asked me how I wanted to be remembered, and my answer was that I wanted to be remembered as intelligent (I am a Leo and I was twenty years old, I need a break, too). My friend was immediately embarrassed and wanted to change his answer. But that was his truth, at that moment, as was mine, in all of its honest glory. My answer to the question has changed many times over the years. I think his may have, too. What is your answer right now, honestly?

■ GODZILLA FOR TEA AT FOUR ■

There certainly are times when we are not at our best and may want to spare people from our gloomy energy. I am learning to accept it, though, as a part of the cycle and part of my truth. I am allowed to be in a bad mood some-times. It took me about thirty years to accept that . . . phew. Sometimes folks can send the energy in a room plummeting simply by their arrival. We may need the shadow side of our energetic selves to push us through situations and onto firmer ground at times. The somber side of us is not necessarily full of "bad" energy. We just have to take care with how we use it. We may discover truth in the reflection. A friend of mine calls my impending dark moods "the tsunami brewing." He likes a bit of warning, if possible. He describes it is as if Rodan or Mothra is about to appear on the scene in an old Japanese horror movie: it turns quiet and an ominous feeling sets in, then the crickets stop chirping, the cat slinks away, the fog gets denser, the music comes up, and suddenly all the cars are streaming away from Tokyo while he is headed toward the city . . . well, you get the picture. All sides of us are our truth, part of the whole complex package. I have become aware that my emotional tsunami usually precedes a whirlwind of creative activity and productive work. Love the lessons to be learned. Now that I understand that, I'm much more open to seeing what happens next rather than fighting it or trying to make it "better." Try not to censor your moods or emotions. The sooner we get to know and accept all the dimensions of our truth, the easier we will be able to use the data to maximize our strengths, potential, and ultimately our joy.

■ RATTLING THE CAGE ■

Our belief systems are given to us by our tribes, our clans, our families, and our cultures. We are told or shown by example what to believe from birth— how to act, what is right, and what is wrong. Most of these belief systems have long histories within families or clans and may not have changed much over time. The roots and expectations run deep. This makes it all the more difficult to pull up that now huge old oak tree in the yard and plant something new in its place. Honoring one's family may keep the peace and order in one's world, but ultimately responding with silence when confronted with beliefs you yourself cannot embrace will wreak havoc with your inner world order. There may not always be something to challenge, but it is worth exploring the questions.

If I listened to everyone who had ideas for what I should be, I would be selling real estate, running a catering business, and teaching high school. But guess what? I have incorporated interests and talents into my life without making any of them my sole career. I have made some money buying and selling houses at the right time, which has allowed me to write and work in film. I love cooking and do so for friends and family with complete joy. I continue to work with adolescents on a volunteer basis because they are so extraordinary and teach me so much. I didn't say anything about it being easy, but it is your life to make it what you most want. Does any of this ring true for you? Challenge your assumptions. Which pieces work for you and which do not seem to be in sync with who you are or want to be? Spiritual curiosity didn't kill the cat, but spiritual complacency just might. Start rattling.

■ STORY: PASSINGS ■

A high school classmate of mine's mother died when we were fourteen. I vividly remember going to the funeral held in an African American church in town. It was my first experience with death. I was overwhelmed by the music, the joy, and the singing, the crying, and screaming. People were collapsing in the aisles and praying out loud. The emotions were raw and loud and messy, in your face, and filled every atom of space in the church.

I grew to learn that when there is a death in my culture, we are asked to act what I think of as counterintuitively. We are encouraged to grieve silently and neatly in public. Funerals become strange, orchestrated performances, with everyone assigned a role, with specific expectations. I remember my father telling my sister, brother, and me before my mother's memorial service that we must keep it together and be strong because all eyes were upon us. I think that my father was saying it more for himself, but we were all on pretty shaky emotional ground at the time.

Grief is unpredictable and sneaks up on you when you least expect it and sends you reeling months and years later. Every new loss becomes a whole new bundle of pain and confusion. It compounds old losses and brings the pain sailing back in under your skin and tugs at the sutures of a shattered heart. People must be allowed to grieve in their own way and in their own time, but it can be confusing when your tribal traditions don't fit with your own emotions.

My animal companion of fourteen years died just recently. I haven't had such an intense and painful loss since losing my mother almost fifteen years ago. My intention for Lil's passing was to be as present as possible—tuned in to her, the grief, and also the gratitude for our time together. It was my chance to witness her life and her death in the same moment. I gathered animal fetishes to accompany her, a favorite photo from the mountain we loved to hike for remembrance, and dog biscuits for the journey. I lit candles and burned piñon incense in honor of our finding each other in New Mexico. I sat with her before the vet came. I cried deeply and kissed her on the nose as I let her go. It was a profound and remarkably peaceful moment as she passed on, and the ritual I created kept me solidly in the moment. It changed my perspective on death and has helped strengthen my desire to be present and to fully participate in life's experiences and offerings. The lessons in loss are profound.

We have an opportunity to learn from each challenging emotional experience if we open our hearts and allow ourselves to feel everything. Loss is indeed a huge one. At times I am reminded of that funeral in the city long ago and wonder at the glory of such a tremendous way to grieve, give thanks for, and celebrate a life.

■ EXERCISE: CHALLENGE YOUR BELIEFS ■

Take a look at all that has formed you. Your world outlook—and, more important, your inward outlook—may be profoundly affected. Start there because that will influence everything else. Changing your beliefs means simply changing your mind—what you hold as the truth, your truth.

Challenge your belief system and definition of self given to you by your family, society, and yourself up to this very point. Question what you know and what you think you know or have been told. Math didn't come easy for you in school, so you shouldn't even consider certain jobs. You've always wanted to play the drums, but you are too old to learn. You aren't thin enough to feel beautiful? Who made up these rules, and why are we accepting them as the truth?

What do you believe at your very core? Listen carefully to the small voice, for it might be whispering softly. What have you been told to believe that you have always questioned and never reconciled in your heart? What do you know?

ACCEPTANCE

When you come to a place of understanding of who you are and where you are now, you will likely be able to let out a sigh of relief. The jig is up, and now you just have to keep breathing and find acceptance for what you have uncovered. How you have used your energy in the past brought you to where you are now. It is all up to you. You can react/act the same way, or you can do things differently. We are still talking about micromovements—minishifts in your mind, body, and spirit are all that is required to begin.

■ You Are the Smartest One ■

If you decide to take action from your place of truth, you may be stirring things up a bit. Other people in your life may not like the outcome, especially if they get left behind. You will first need courage to give yourself permission to be the person you discover you are. Ask yourself if you are willing to surrender to trust and to accept the changes that unfold, even if they don't look exactly how you thought they would.

What you have done in the past, how you have responded in situations, brings you to this very moment. You have another chance if past actions and reactions have not brought you to where you had hoped. Recognize when/why you do what you do, and then decide if it is a pattern that serves you. You must be getting something out of it, or you wouldn't keep doing it.

If you come to realize that the only benefit is a familiar action and reaction, then this work may be difficult. If you are going to make changes, then you are going to have to let some things go. Making room for the energy changes means letting go of some emotional attachments that use up your energy. Letting go of friendships or relationships that no longer support the path you are on is very difficult. Some you may have to do abruptly, and some may just fade away. Know that you will have setbacks and lousy moments, but don't be too hard on yourself. Keep bringing yourself back to your truth and where you are headed. Listen to your own advice. Would you let a friend stay in a bad relationship or a job that she hated without encouraging her to make changes and then talking through the possibilities? I don't think so. It is the same if someone offers you help. There is no shame or weakness in accepting help, whether it is monetary or emotional support, or a connection to someone or something. We extend offers to our friends and loved ones, and yet when the tables are turned, we may be reluctant to accept help in return. No fair changing the rules. It may feel awkward at first, but try to let go of all that energy you are expending feeling uncomfortable and just let it in and let it help.

We may struggle to live without judgment of others, but we have to admit it isn't an easy task. I felt infinitely better for my lack of perfection in that department when a friend told me about a nun she knew who also struggled not to be judgmental. I figured I was in good company. The sister told my friend that when she finds herself being judgmental, she tries to find one thing positive to say about the person or situation she has issues with. When you are critical of someone, realize that it is usually due to jealousy or some kind of guilt about a similar situation in your own life. Try holding up that mirror when you sit in judgment of someone else. You may be surprised at how familiar that face is peeking back at you.

■ A Word from Buddha ■

The Buddha's words "Your work is to discover your work and then with all your heart give yourself to it" liberated me. I now interpret the word "work" to mean your truth, the undeniable you. I am not talking about figuring out whether you should be an accountant or a firefighter. Your work is how you are in the world. Your work is who you are and what you are bringing to the table in this life. That is what we are all on the path to discover. Rereading Buddha's words recently gave me an "ah ha" moment. For years I have struggled with the notion of my truth and who I am. I have always been told that I am fun to have around. It is true that I will try my hardest to make you laugh, especially if you are crabby. In a college interview years ago, I was asked to describe myself with one word. I chose "approachable." Almost twenty years later I think I would give the same answer. I genuinely like interacting with people, so it must be mixed in with some of the energy I send out there.

I played on the tennis team in college and I think most of the reason why I kept making the team was that I was kind of fun to have around. It certainly wasn't for my killer serve or fierce competitive spirit. My coach even had to stop me from saying, "Nice shot," to my opponents throughout the matches I played. I am usually good in an interview and often despaired that was how I got all of my jobs. For the longest time I struggled with that idea. Did I have any real skills or a place in the world? Who you are is the biggest part of your skill set, I discovered. And then my "ah ha" moment happened.

I had just met someone I was interested in getting to know and was talking to my friend Ann Marie about the situation. I said that I was afraid that I was being "too much" and maybe I terrified him because I can be such a bulldozer of energy when I meet people and feel a connection to them. She stopped me right there and said, "There is never too much Hailey; in fact, there is probably never enough." And here was my "ah ha" moment combined with rereading Buddha's words. Our work is our energetic contribution to the mix. Maybe I am supposed be someone that is easy to be around. Maybe that is my work in life? Maybe that is what I am supposed to do with all my heart? Maybe I am supposed to be a bulldozer or a safe harbor for the other travelers, even for just a moment. And does it bring me joy? Yes, indeed, especially when I remember boundaries. That is the work I must do with a passion. That is how I need to be in the world. Whatever work I do for a living will be infused with that energy if that is indeed my truth. Not an easy thing to do every day, I admit, but what an epiphany. It is important that the "must be" should come from your own desires, not other people's "should be." Discovering and accepting your own truth is very liberating, if you act in harmony with the person you discover.

■ DAYS WHEN THE RAINS CAME ■

There are the days you can't handle being in the world and want to be invisible. And they will happen at some point during this process. You don't even want to be in the presence of your conscious self and aren't comfortable in your own skin. Transformation and growth can be unsettling. Some days "responsibility" is the dirtiest word you have ever heard. It is so impossibly hard to get out of bed. In fact, why bother? What are they going to do, fire me? They can find someone else to drive the car pool to school today. So what if I cancel that lunch meeting at the last minute? There are those days. Something will happen today that will make you sad or angry that you got out of bed, you know that. Wouldn't it be better to know that something, many things in fact, will bring us joy today if we will only look for them?

We do have days that catch us off guard, when we wake up not only on the wrong side of the bed but pretty much underneath it, wrapped in the blankets and sheets. Maybe we should just lie there and see what happens. Someone might come by with a cup of coffee and a note to the world excusing our absence. Maybe we should struggle like crazy to free ourselves. Some days the next step may seem so very clear, and on days when the rains come we may not have even a hint. Each time you get through these days, if you have paused to consider them, you will have stockpiled more ammunition for shooting your way out of the next one, hopefully with less fleeting results than Butch and Sundance. Maybe on days when the rains come, we should stand outside, get soaking wet, and go stomp in a few puddles. That ought to create a big old energy shift. The ammunition is made up of equal parts of joy and abandon.

■ RELATIONSHIPS . . . OY! ■

I am not covering new ground talking about the challenge of being in relationships—love, business, familial, friendship, or all of the above. We know relationships are complex and fill us alternately with joy and dread, depending on the hour of the day. We may strive to devise a plan to merge our steamer trunks' worth of emotional baggage together in a way we can all survive and thrive. Sometimes it does help to understand why we go off the deep end when our pens are not all back in the holder on our desk exactly the way we left them, or all our buttons get pushed (with both hands at once) when they forget our birthday or shut down communication lines, or sound just like our parents. One friend of mine said about her long-term relationship, "No one loves or hates him every day more than I do, not even God." It has to be healthy and liberating that there are indeed days when we cannot bear the sight of each other for one minute longer. Sometimes we just aren't in sync;

we turn our filters on high and hear everything they say sideways. Those are the days it is probably best to keep our thoughts to ourselves, though, unless of course we feel the need to pick a fight and stir things up. At least understand why you are doing it, the real reason, not the one you end up yelling at them for. Then accept them for who they are, not who they aren't in your eyes, and remember something good about them. If the time comes to pack it up and move on, you will hear it first from down deep inside. Honor that voice when you can—you know it won't fail you.

■ SOUL PEEKING OUT ■

Can we all make a promise to try never to ask anyone, "So, what do you do?" again? There is so much pressure involved in that question. We may as well ask, "So, how do you justify your existence in the world?" It is loaded with angst-producing enzymes, I am sure. It is hard not to define ourselves by what makes us money, but that is not who we are, it is just what we do. Let's not confuse the two. The world is askew in what we have decided to value. It may make it more difficult to offer our true selves to the world. Find the courage when you can. It will become easier with each small step you take or wish you attach a desire to. Be gentle with one another, too. We are all lurching and tiptoeing and dancing here together. There are bound to be some collisions.

Most days I let the real me out, and some days I hide her in a box under my bed. If someone tries coaxing her out with a friendly inquiry, she is more likely to make an appearance. Next time you meet someone for the first time, try asking him: "So, what do you do that makes you happy?" I think that question will tell you more about who he really is. You can't imagine people's reactions to that question. Their whole face changes, and the force fields usually melt on the spot. Most of us have never been asked that question. Try it. It is a great way to get to know people, and they are not likely to forget you anytime soon. Ask people in your life that question, too. You may be surprised at the answers they offer you. You may reveal a whole new side of them. Give them permission to let their real selves peek out from the box under their bed. Yours will, too.

■ STORY: EASING INTO UNDERSTANDING ■

Joseph is in his mid-sixties. He is physically healthy and working as a consultant. His wife started her own business a few years ago that is now beginning to see a profit. They have planned well, so they are financially stable. Their children are grown and have families of their own. Joseph came to me with chronic lower back pain and a general feeling of anxiety. He wasn't quite sure where the anxiety stemmed from at that point. We talked first about his life and any concerns that might be weighing on him. Retirement was his greatest concern. Joseph had been the sole provider for his family. He now worked independently after leaving a company he had been with for many years. He was not being forced to retire. His work had always involved travel and kept him away from home a great deal, and he was growing tired of that. He had reached a level of expertise in his field and was very highly regarded by his peers. He was worried about what came next. What would he do with himself if he retired? Would he be seen by others as a useless old man?

These are difficult concerns facing many people on the verge of retirement. Many of us have been defined by our work for many years, and suddenly that changes. We may think we have to find a new identity, in essence. Or do we? I wanted Joseph to look at what parts of him and parts of his life would be changing if he retired. What did he want to change? I had him work on an outline of his biography, noting all the pivotal points in his life and significant events, accomplishments, and failures. When and where was he the happiest? Why? I asked him to put descriptions of himself with the events as we went through it. Over and over again the word "responsible" came up throughout the events in his life, in his family helping to take care of his brothers and sisters after his father died, when he was in the military during the Korean War, providing for his own family, and building his business career and in civic involvement. He was the one everyone looked to for strength, but this now made him tired, not inspired. We also talked about other areas of his life besides work that brought him joy and made him feel good. Seeing this helped Joseph come to terms with his fears about retirement. He did retire and was almost immediately asked to advise a local business on increasing its productivity. Other businesses have called, but he is going to take it one step at a time and travel with his wife and maybe build that wooden boat he always dreamed of, because this is what he really wants to do.

■ EXERCISE: BIOGRAPHY OF THE SOUL ■

If you were to write your soul's biography, what would it say? What gives you blissful, over-the-moon joy? What makes you weep from way, way down deep? How do you love—conditionally, frugally, or with your biggest self? Is there faith in your soul, and what does it look like? Ponder awhile on what you might look like on the inside. What is stirring or lying dormant buried within? Is yours a gracious, or greedy, soul? Fulfilled, or yearning? What do you value in yourself? What is hidden down deep that never has had a voice?

Take some time to ponder these questions, sit with them, and then respond with pen and paper, or however you are moved.

ACTION, MOMENTUM, IMPACT

Some nights, stay up until dawn,
As the moon sometimes does for the sun.
Be a full bucket pulled up the dark way
of a well, then lifted out into the light.

Something opens our wings. Something
makes boredom and hurt disappear.
Someone fills the cup in front of us.
We taste only sacredness.

■ □ ■

—Unknown

ACTION

■□■□■□■□■□■□■□■□■□■□■□■□■□■□■□■□□■

Notice that I didn't put this chapter at the beginning of the book. It may seem to many to be the first step in making a change, but only if that action is changing how you think and feel about your life. Some of you may be tempted to see the term "action" and jump into overachiever mode and set off a tornado of change. Some of you may see the term and want to go back and hide under your bed, trembling. Somehow I don't think it will make you cringe, because you have come this far in the book. You have been on a path of action simply by thinking about situations differently. Keep the changes small either way. Make the step, take the bite. You have been in training to reshape and refocus your emotional and spiritual reactions to your life. Ask yourself which realms of your life feel strongest right now: spiritual, physical, or emotional. What area needs the most support? You can support the weak area by taking risks and pushing yourself in another.

■ SNEAKING UP ON CHANGE ■

Working to put all areas of our life in sync or in harmony is a daily endeavor. You have to understand your body, its limits and its limitations, as well as those of your spirit and your mind. Challenging and building strength in your physical self as well as spiritual self gives you more tools for when the randomness happens. Chaos is the order in our everyday universe. That isn't necessarily a bad thing. If you are feeling overwhelmed in one area of life, then try pushing yourself in another.

A woman I know spent years taking care of her mother and then her grandchildren for some time. As much as she loved it most of the time, it was emotionally and spiritually draining for her. She decided to start working with a personal trainer to become physically stronger. The physical realm was where she thought she could push herself in order to feel more in balance. Her attitude about the situation changed dramatically, and she found herself with a much higher energy level and new emotional perspective. That is sneaking up on change. Talking about the anxiety she had about the situation and the fatigue she felt was not the remedy for her to shift the energy around the circumstances. That just kept her focused on the problem, not the solution. She had to access it from another approach, seemingly unrelated but actually very much so. You have to figure out what area can carry a bit more of the weight in order to tip life back into balance.

When training physically, you push yourself for a certain number of days in a row and then take one or two off. When you go back to it, you are stronger than ever. Change is like that—your mind may be way ahead of the rest of you, skipping to the desired end result. You can work slowly though and maybe take steps you hadn't anticipated to get where you want to be. Your thoughts and spiritual energy are already working for you. Understand what your body can do—and your mind and spirit, what their limits are—and push yourself a little bit further the next time. Many of us do not get challenged or often put ourselves in spiritually challenging situations. Spiritually and emotionally challenging events happen to us all the time and often unexpectedly, like the deaths of loved ones, new jobs, retirement, and relationships. Unhappiness is a spiritual challenge, not something to accept. What tools can we use to deal with the wounding of our soul if we are not spiritually fit? It takes courage and faith to keep the momentum going. Trying to undo what you may think is a mistake may make the waters muddier; move forward from there, to the essence of truth. Discover the insight that shows you that it is not always better to go back and try to fix things, but instead to go forward and do it differently the next time. Taking spiritual and emotional risks can bring powerful lessons and strength.

■ FIND THAT THING ■

We are the only ones ultimately responsible for how we are in the world, how far we push ourselves, how much we learn, and how much we give and accept love and abundance. I discovered many life lessons while working with teenagers at a psychiatric facility and in several different mentoring programs. Working with teens provides me with interesting challenges and great joy. They have helped me to grasp a very simple belief that applies to all of us, at any age. If we have at least one thing in our life that we are passionate about, pursue, give ourselves to, and make a part of us, then we will always have a true source of strength.

The teens I worked with who were involved with sports or a club or played an instrument or had a passionate interest in a hobby were the ones who could better handle all the changes being thrown their way. These activities became their refuge, a safe place to retreat to. They always had one place where they belonged, where they fit in, where they could shine. It became my mission with every teenager I worked with to discover what they were passionate about. What did they want to know everything about and what did they want to be good at? What situations or activity gave them peace or made them feel strong and safe? The answers are the key to beginning a dialogue with them and gaining their trust in building a relationship.

I will tell you what I tell them: find one thing that you love or want to be good at and devour it. Find the one skill or interest that you can push yourself to be really good at, care about, or talk about with knowledge and enthusiasm, that you can be proud of. One thing will lead to all things and will lead you to a life you love. I don't want to hear the excuse that you are too old or that it is too late. Think about what you love to do or have forgotten that you loved. It doesn't go away. That passion may be dormant but still present. If you challenge yourself and take risks in these realms of desire, then you become used to triumphs and disappointments as you go along. Each time you heal stronger. It will make it easier to deal with the advances and setbacks in other areas of your life. It will give you confidence and strength. You are creating one corner of the world that is yours alone and one that you will always have, no matter if everyone or everything else abandons you. If I am struggling with a challenge, my friend M tells me to go cook something fabulous or at least to pretend I am in the kitchen. The kitchen is where I am most confident, where I take risks with abandon and glee. If I can put myself in "cooking mode" and just remember how free and confident I feel there, it always helps carry that strength into the situation I may be struggling with.

All parts of your life are connected. Discover or remember which arena you shine in and keep pushing yourself to be better or know more. This fosters a greater knowledge of self, which spills over into our emotional, spiritual, and physical lives. This is the place where faith grows and carries us through. Go to those places, real and in your mind, that bring you joy. Your true power lies within.

Imagine if we could find our sources of inspiration and courage when we are young. We would learn to love going against the norm and being true to ourselves. We would have more strength for adversity and change that comes our way throughout our lives. We could welcome change. We would have the inner knowing that we can find a way through the dark night because we know who we are. Even if we are not sure what our limits are, we would have a confidence that we could somehow handle what rains down upon us. It is never too late to discover confidence with room for questions and mistakes and missteps, and the ability to pick up and move on with ease instead of angst. Change happens whether or not we stand still or charge ahead. Finding ways to ride the ebb and flow of momentum is mighty wisdom. Getting to a point where we can stand in the midst of chaos and say, "It is what it is," and not look around to place the blame on someone or something is a place of inspiration, a place of knowing, a place of joy.

■ STORY: A PASSION FOR BOOKS ■

All of the adolescents I worked with in the classroom at the psychiatric unit were special. One girl will stay with me forever. She was tall and strong and loud and intimidated some people. Everyone warned me before she came into my room that she would be disruptive and possibly violent. Angela (not her real name) was fifteen when I met her and had already been through many unimaginable events in her short life. Her mother was addicted to drugs and was in and out of rehabilitation facilities and jail. One, if not several, of her mother's boyfriends had sexually abused and beaten Angela. Needless to say, she didn't trust people and felt very vulnerable. She was indeed loud and disruptive, but all in an effort to get people to like her. She was very engaging with a quick smile. I knew I would have to figure out a way to diffuse some of the negative attention-seeking behavior but also build her confidence and trust.

So, I discovered what her passion was. She loved to read. Books were Angela's solace and escape. Her favorite book was *The Secret Garden*, but she devoured everything she could find. It was her connection to fantasy and a place of beauty and security. Her own world was pretty hard to look at and must have been even harder to be a part of. I asked Angela to be the librarian for the class. If anyone wanted to check out a book, they had to go to her first. Angela was thrilled. She took the job very seriously and began to calm down in the classroom. Angela was the queen of the books and controlled that kingdom. She organized a system for signing out the books and stayed focused. Books were her connection to good emotions, and as the librarian for the class, she was given authority around the subject she loved. Angela created sacred space with her books, and no one could "get" her there when she was reading or overseeing the library.

Due to insurance and hospital policies (don't get me started), we had the children for increasingly shorter periods of time for cognitive evaluation and assessment. I was devastated when Angela was transferred just when she was settling in and doing good work. One of my wise and compassionate colleagues offered me a tremendous lesson that day. He told me that Angela would always have that period of trust and caring to hang on to, no matter what, that it was now a resource for her. The connection had been imprinted in her memory. Hopefully she would remember that someone in the world thought she was special and smart and worthwhile. And she would always have her books and her passionate identity as a reader. When life was challenging, she could draw upon that emotional strength and source of knowing. It was and is my prayer for Angela that she does. My own awakening to the understanding of how powerful our reservoirs of spiritual and emotional strength can be was born that moment.

■ EXERCISE: DO THREE THINGS ■

Now you are ready to take an action step. Let's try small bites first. The important part of this step is building the momentum of change. Small changes are never insignificant. You have chosen to walk a new path by reading this book. You can't ever go back to the place you were.

Once a week do three things you have been thinking of doing: meditate for five minutes more, or for the first time, try a new recipe, buy purple socks, sew the button on your jacket, return the library books, draw a picture, throw those scary things in your refrigerator away, repot a plant, join the gym or a yoga class, call an old friend, take a drive to a new town, renew your passport. Allow yourself to do things you want to do. Be spontaneous—whatever has been on your list or taking up space in your head. It doesn't matter how small or trivial you may think the task or activity is if it is something you have wanted to do. We are going for small accomplishments, just getting things done and making space for other changes. Do the three things throughout the course of one day. This will encourage you to welcome change and achievement at work, at home, in contemplation, and in life. Three small achievements carry power and will trigger a flow of confidence and change. Ready, go.

MOMENTUM

It is likely our fears have been tagging along, nipping at our heels on this journey. Keeping them at bay enough to carry on and not get thrown off track will take effort. They especially like to show up in the middle of a journey when we may not be paying attention or figure they have lost our trail. No such luck. They may be drooling on your shoes as we speak. It is similar to reaching a physical fitness plateau. It may take a big push to keep the momentum going and to shake off the worry and doubt.

■ WHAT IS THE WORST (BEST) THAT CAN HAPPEN? ■

A friend taught me an exercise that I have used when I find fear holding me back or I am at a crossroads. She told me to ask one question of the situation, "What is the worst that can happen?" If the answer is the likelihood I will be maimed if I take the step I am considering, I might reconsider my choices. Usually when I ask myself that question, however, the potential consequence is often something pretty tame, like an ego bruise or misstep for the "bloopers" reel. So what if you are embarrassed? It is so fleeting. Aren't you proud for trying? If someone gets temporarily angry with you for speaking the truth, have faith that it will be resolved and will strengthen the relationship if you spoke from the heart. If one person says no, maybe the next will say yes. Discover that part of faith that reminds you that every experience, both joyous or challenging, will change you and the universe.

If you ask yourself, What is the worst that can happen? let that be the quieter question so that it doesn't become an excuse to stand still. Then start asking yourself, What is the best that can happen if I make this change? Dwell there for a while when you answer. Roll around in the fantasy, gnaw on the prospects. That is where you want to focus your energy, on the exciting possibilities.

■ RITUAL VS. ROUTINE ■

Ritual implies transition, movement, and change. Rituals establish us in the moment, in the present, but push us forward with unknown results. Rituals created with thoughtful intention can help us maintain the focus and momentum of change. Routine is fixed. There is a desirability for sameness, an expected outcome. We all have our routines, for we are indeed creatures of habit. We buy coffee at the same shop and try to sit in the same seat on the train to work. We always use the same treadmill at the gym, maintain everyday routines with our children, and drive or walk the same paths to and from places. This is not a negative occurrence. We likely create these daily routines because it gives us a sense of comfort and balance in our days, a sameness and predictability. We can control these routines and modify or change them to our specifications. We are in charge. We are in control. This predictability may indeed provide comfort and a chance to feel at ease for a small portion of an otherwise hectic and unpredictable day.

■ FREE DOG WITH FILL-UP ■

But look what can happen if we change our routine and become open to all the possibilities. I have lived in the same town for two and a half years and have always gone to the same gas station, even though it isn't the closest or always the cheapest—just the routine. One cold evening recently as I was going to get gas, I drove into another station. I can't explain why. As I was waiting for the attendant, I noticed a fat black Lab wagging her tail to be let in to the warmer office. No one seemed to be paying much attention to her. I couldn't resist getting out and going over to play with her. When the attendant came out I said, "What a great dog you have." He said, "Do you want her? She was abandoned." I couldn't believe it. That night I talked to the man who had been taking care of her there. He couldn't keep her and was looking for a good home for her. We met the next day and it was a love connection with Whitney and me right away. I brought the wonderfully sweet and funny dog home that morning. What a joyous event. And all because I changed my routine. I have to add a note here. That very morning as I walked on the beach, I had asked the question to the sea, "I wonder if I will ever find as wonderful a companion dog as Lil?" The energy I had focused on that question was clear and strong, because look who showed up. The universe worked quickly to grant my wish and lined up the circumstances perfectly.

Routine can be a time of meditative solace in an overwhelming sensory habitat that is our daily lives, it is true. There is the risk of complacency or rigidity setting in if we get too settled into our routines, however. It can carry over into our spiritual lives and affect communication, self-awareness, and receptiveness to change. Routine isn't a dirty word unless it becomes psychically and spiritually synonymous with "stuck." Rituals can become routines, events unfolding with the same outcome unless someone within makes a shift.

▪ YOU'RE A SLY ONE, MR. GRINCH ▪

Holidays can be so emotionally charged because of the threat or promise of repeated ritual routines. They come around again and we swear that this year it is going to be different, or we groan and give in to the fact that it will always be the same. We get locked into behavior that we have a hard time breaking free of, with family especially. We each have a specific role in the tribe, and anticipated behavior is accepted and expected. No one likes change in those situations because that would force everyone to look at his own life and patterns and throw the whole system out of balance. Everyone would then have to make energy shifts in response. Once again, if you make one change in the system, the whole system changes. You can suggest a change in venue or menu and give everyone a new role, a new responsibility. The easiest piece to change is the energy that you put toward the situation. Maybe you can experience the event in a whole new light if you simply change your mind and change your focus.

Rituals can be created to mark passages or transitions in life. Rituals make us aware and force us to stay in the present while influencing the momentum of energy shifts. We can key in to the momentum created by initial or desired changes in our life by designing rituals that complement the process. Rituals are not all religious or involve elaborate ceremony. Rituals can be habits of thought as well. The process begins with some kind of calling from the silence. Somewhere we connect with ourselves that desire or need for energy shifts. We must be willing to quiet the noise and access our desires for change. This action requires reaching inward to our true, authentic selves and trusting the guidance we may trigger. Listen to your intuitive voice when creating rituals.

■ CHANGE AT EYE LEVEL ■

My friend Kay was married to Paul for many years. At a point in time their relationship as husband and wife came to an end. Kay is 5'5" and Paul is 6'4". As a transition ritual after the divorce was final, Kay invited a friend over for some wine and some redecorating. Kay was going to stay in the house that she and Paul had shared. Kay wanted and needed to reclaim her space. Her intention was to change the energy in the house to better suit her new situation. She wanted to make it hers as a newly single woman. Kay and Paul had lived in the space for years collecting art and objects and creating a home. Kay was going to have to make some changes in order to feel like it was now her space. The first act was to rehang all the pictures in the house. Paul had hung them all, and they were from his perspective, more than a foot higher than Kay's. Kay brought the art back into her world by rehanging it. She made it more a part of her world and claimed her space with her art at eye level—her eye level. The art was now accessible to her field of vision and more a part of her every day. What may seem like a simple change was very significant. This simple ritual changed the energy in Kay's space and made her feel more connected and comfortable during the emotional transition. Changes we make and rituals we create to accompany the process do not have to be major to impact how they make us feel.

Daily awareness and the creation of rituals will give you strength in times of challenge or adversity and keep you in the present. Just the way you can ask more from your body under challenging physical situations if you are healthy and fit, so can you ask more from your soul if your spirit is in good shape. Rituals feed our spirits, make us aware, and support movement.

■ CREATING RITUALS ■

What can we expect to happen when we create rituals for our lives and strive for internal alterations? Will we find more joy, productivity, inspiration, money in our bank account? Hopefully, to the first three, and maybe to the last. There is no doubt that you will feel the energy shifts when you create and conduct the rituals, which may indeed lead to increases in all areas. After all, clarity and desire make room for creativity and delight. They push aside the fear and allow action and movement in. Nothing at all happens without action and movement, for then we are just responding to others' energy shifts and not participating in the energy flow, except as a spectator caught up in the wave. The action can be simply taking the familiar negative thought and turning it into a positive one. Rituals ground us in the present and carry us to the future. The change of seasons are a logical time to create rituals for transition. Many cultures and spiritual societies have rituals and ceremonies built around planting and harvesting cycles, the phases of the moon, and the solstices. Rituals can reconnect us with memories and emotions. A friend of mine lights candles on Friday evening, the Jewish Sabbath, mainly because of her memories of how special the ritual was to her mother. Each week she lights the candles and takes time to remember her mother.

■ STORY: MOVING ON ■

Alex was ending a longtime on-again, off-again relationship and was having trouble letting go all the way. It didn't help that her ex kept sending her books with manipulative inscriptions that made her feel terrible. She called me one day and asked if I would help her design a ritual to let go of the old relationship and give her clear energy and room for her new relationship. As we talked she showed me a book the ex had recently sent her. The title page was filled with a long diatribe about her not being the woman she always said she wanted to be and how it was too bad she couldn't live up to those ideals of being an honorable person. Oy! What a productive way to try to win someone back: guilt. Please. The manipulation made me feel angry, too, and secretly my first thought was to throw the book across the room.

Alex had the book in her retreat room, where she did yoga and meditated and painted. Every time she came into the room, her eyes and her mind went straight to that book on the shelf. There it sat, taunting her. This threw her off balance and shut down her creativity and focus. Clearly the book had to go, but how to do it without anger and too much emotional energy? Also, I don't know about you, but I generally can't throw away or destroy books. Books have mighty mojo. You just don't do it.

Alex said she was tired of feeling guilty and responsible for ruining his life by choosing to move on with her own life. I asked her to sit quietly for a few minutes and think about the good parts of the relationship, the lessons, and then to see if she was in a quieter, less angry place. I then suggested she rip the page he had written on out of the book and burn it. And finally to further change the energy of the book, I told her that I would love to read it and asked if she would mind giving it to me as a gift? I would hold on to it for her. She cried and laughed and gladly handed me the book. Alex initiated the process of letting go of the guilt and anger of the old relationship and made room for the new one. She reclaimed her private retreat space, rediscovering a place for contemplation and creativity.

■ EXERCISE: CREATING RITUALS ■

Create rituals for times of transition or celebration or for everyday life. Ask a friend or family members to participate, if appropriate. The event does not have to be anything grandly significant. It can be a celebration of letting go of a negative aspect of your life or any small success or triumph of spirit. Celebrate a friendship or honor the memory of a loved one. Take the time to decide what is right for the occasion, and have clear intentions and an open heart and mind. Plan your ritual in conjunction with a natural occurrence, if that appeals to you.

Some of the ingredients you may want to use in your rituals are candles and incense, nature or natural surroundings, if you have a connection to the outdoors, and any touchstones or talismans relating to your occasion. Add music, poetry, art, or dance to your ceremony. Songs and the spoken word can be very meaningful also. Stay focused on your intention. If you want to be supported in letting go of an attachment to a situation, you may want to write down what it is that you want to let go and then burn it in a candle. Or just say it out loud. One thing to remember is that rituals are never created or carried out in anger, but with introspection and humility. When I create rituals at the beach, I may write what I want to let go of on a piece of paper and burn it to release it to the world in the smoke. Any hopes or dreams I want to attract I burn and then throw into the water, with the idea that the tide will carry it back to me. There is no one way to create rituals. Discover what has meaning for you.

If you look, you'll find
truth etched on the tree trunk,
the shark's tooth, a shell, a hunk
of root and soil. Study from beginning to end.
Alpha and omega—these are the cirrus alphabet,
the Gnostics' cloudy "so—and yet."

■ □ ■

from "Natural Theology"
—Kelly Cherry

IMPACT

■□■□■□■□■□■□■□■□■□■□■□■□■□■□■□■■□■

You may be aware now of the momentum of change intensifying in some or all areas of your life. Realizing what has changed in your world may hit you in the face or reveal itself over time. Now that the momentum has begun, how can you stay on the path? What can you do to follow through to this conclusion and then on to whatever comes next? As we now see, change does not begin with the physical action. It began in your heart and soul way back. Your desired or fantasized outcome may not happen fast enough, or at all. It will not happen if you whisper in the same breath, "I want, but I don't think I can have or be . . . " You will have to remain open and receptive to shifts you may not have anticipated. Change may show up in a different package or costume than the one you consciously ordered. This is where the awareness skills you have been developing and understanding come into play.

■ GOOD ORDER ■

While you are taking risks and making changes in your physical, emotional, or spiritual worlds, events you don't consciously initiate will occur. You will have to adapt to change that happens to you, unplanned or unexpected life events or traumas. Don't try to control every last detail, or you may miss the most interesting parts. Some of your usual routines may no longer serve this path, either. At this point, you have better self-awareness and understanding on your side—tools to keep the good order. Conjure up times in your life when you have taken risks. Remember how it felt, the exhilaration and anticipation. The good order is a confidence that you will be able to handle whatever comes your way. Maybe not always with grace or without getting a little banged up emotionally, but able to get through.

Because we cannot predict exactly how our energy shifts will be responded to, we will have to look at their impact with an open mind. Changes may not happen when or exactly how we hope. It will fall into place the way it should be, which may not be how you pictured it. Be ready to be surprised and to respond thoughtfully. There is important information contained in all energy responses. Maybe you will find yourself simply more open to the color blue. Maybe you will find yourself clapping along at a concert for the first time. Maybe you will make eye contact with your mail carrier. Maybe you will plan a trip to Alaska. These are all a result of shifts in energy, and they will impact every part of your life. We may not be able to see the benefits right away or the message contained within, but there are lessons to be learned at each turn.

Impact

When you are assessing the impact of what has shifted for you so far, focus on the overall picture and be aware of even the seemingly smallest of movements. Stay in the present and in your truth.

The seasons are nature's most obvious gift of change and illustration of impact. Plants, animals, and people all respond and adapt to the shifts in our environments and ourselves. Our world slumbers in the diminished light, enduring cold, and monochromatic theme of winter, and our spirits are gently reawakened to a shimmering palette and hope in the spring. Summer brings the lazy, sticky heat and full, 153 of color and settles into the majesty and texture of the autumn landscape in the cycle of the earth's transformation. Nature's impact on our world can be subtle or extreme, but even the smallest changes, like just a few degrees of temperature, can have a lasting and far-reaching impact around the world. Energy shifts you make in your life follow the same pattern. Carl Jung said:

The great events of world history are, at bottom, profoundly unimportant. In the last analysis, the essential thing is the life of the individual. This alone makes history, here alone do the great transformations take place, and the whole history of the world ultimately springs to a giant summation from these hidden sources in individuals. In our most private and subjective lives, we are not only passive witnesses to our age, but also its makers.

We all have a responsibility to understand our ultimate impact on ourselves, one another, and the rest of the world. Use your newfound awareness to notice your evolving impact on your immediate and greater worlds.

■ STORY: MAKING ROOM FOR POSSIBILITY ■

Jim is approaching forty, owns a home, and has a job he enjoys. It pays him well enough to pursue his interests in sports and traveling. He hasn't had a serious relationship in a few years but makes friends with women pretty easily. He said he had been feeling less confident about asking women out and he never invites friends over. Jim has a full life but would like a committed relationship and possibly a family. His sister gave him a gift certificate for a Reiki session, and he arrived with some curiosity and looking for some kind of change in his life. He just wasn't sure where to begin.

I worked to clear some of the energy blocks, and we talked more after the session. He seemed very settled into his routines, from exercise to eating at a few local restaurants and going out during the week and on weekends. He said he rarely varied his schedule.

I asked him to describe his house and where and how he thought another person might fit into the picture. What he described was the perfect setup for a man living alone. The living room was centered on the television with his favorite couch, which he admitted had seen better days quite some time ago. Most of the artwork on the walls was framed posters from college. He said there was rarely anything in the refrigerator because he ate out most of the time, and his bedroom was sparse. Not a very inviting setup for most women.

Jim agreed to spend some quiet time envisioning the life that he wanted and to think about his space. I told him that he didn't have to throw everything away (definitely keep the Foosball table) but to spend some time in his house and see how it felt. He called me a few weeks later and told me he had bought a new couch and a cabinet for the TV. He bought plants and changed the artwork and cleaned out the "junk room" and turned it into a guest room. Jim said he got on a roll and had fun. He felt much more comfortable in his space and eager to invite people over. Jim realized that he hadn't even wanted to spend much time in his space before and that whether or not he met anyone, he was feeling more content and confident. He felt a lot more open to the possibility. He was learning to cook and enjoying his home. Jim had changed the energy in the space he lived in, which in turn carried over to his attitude about inviting people into his home and his life. The physical changes he made in his home had impacted his emotional state.

■ EXERCISE: CHANGE YOUR ROUTINE . . . ■ GO ON, JUST A LITTLE

Now that you are an old pro at creating change in your life, this is the chance to take a look at the routines you live with. Are your routines strict to the point of superstition, or are they flexible and easily altered? Does the idea of changing any of your routines frighten you or make you uneasy? That may be the one to change if it has become an emotional dependence. You don't have to change the routine drastically, just change it somehow and notice what happens. If you usually go shopping at lunchtime, take a walk instead. If you listen to the news on your way to work, listen to music instead. If you always drive the same routes, try a new one. If you do the same exercise routine every day, try a meditation class or lessons in a new sport. And if you have the same fights with your partner about money or sex, try something different.

RETURN, RESURRECTION, ASSESSMENT

And if the earthly no longer knows your name,
whisper to the silent earth: I am flowing.
To the flashing water say: I am.

■ □ ■

from "Sonnets to Orpheus"
—Rainer Maria Rilke

RETURN

■□■□■□■□■□■□■□■□■□■□■□■□■□■□■□■

Throughout this journey you will be confronted with your fears, and while they may shift, they won't likely disappear. Old habits die hard—for everyone. In order to return to familiar physical and emotional surroundings and situations, you may have to create boundaries so that you can maintain your momentum. You have changed but you have to live in the world you left, to a certain degree.

■ A PHOENIX FROM THE ASHES ■

Your return carries you back with a new vibration and a better understanding of yourself and your relationship to the universe. You have changed. You are returning to a world that has not. It will have no choice but to respond to you differently because your energy has shifted, but it won't be easy. The first part of the return journey is a solo trip and will need to avoid situations and places that will try to drag you back. You will hopefully bring with you a newfound or rediscovered courage, a certain amount of emotional evolution, and a much fuller spiritual toolbox.

Your perception of the place you left behind may have changed, but that place may go on as if nothing has changed. People will expect you to respond to them the same way and to behave as before. You may be ready to leave old reactions behind you, but old habits die hard—for you and for everyone you are in relationship with. You may have to create boundaries, either temporary or permanent, to protect yourself emotionally. You will have to call upon your new-found inner strength to carry you through. This is one of the big hard parts.

Meanwhile, you may be spit back emotionally bruised and a bit chewed up but on the other side of spiritual transformation and enlightenment. And ultimately you will have arrived stronger. You will be defining your new place in the world. Letting go of familiar habits and ways of seeing yourself in the world is an uneasy road. Most spiritual growth journeys are challenging on many levels. Reaching any kind of enlightenment involves a process of letting go or death—certain thoughts, emotions, and beliefs must die in order for you to be reborn, a reformed being. No one ever said birth the first time around was an easy process, so rebirth, complicated by our conscious fears and active self-doubt, is not going to be a cakewalk. We hopefully emerge able to integrate new knowledge and will adopt more conscious, clear, and peaceful dance steps. The tentative and wobbly steps of a newborn colt may be more on target—they are crucial, new life steps. You will have walked fire and come through a spiritual rite of passage. You must trust the emergence of your new self and continue to question and explore your path and journey as you travel on. Depend on yourself to stay true to your dreams.

Many cultures have rites of passage or rituals for transition and transformation woven through their traditions. Rites of passage challenge you at every turn and may make you very, very afraid. This is not the same kind of fear that paralyzes you and keeps you stuck in dissatisfying situations, unproductive relationships, or harmful behavior patterns. It is the other side of that fear, the kind that inspires and motivates you out of that stranded place.

One man shared with me his own experience of a formal rite of passage after participating in his first Sun Dance. Sun Dances last for many days and nights and are physically and emotionally challenging at extraordinary levels. His obligation is to dance four times in his life:

Perhaps like others I have talked to, after the first test, you begin to see your true weaknesses, you replay your old angers, fall prey to vices, and see more in yourself you don't like (in recognition to the high bar of commitment that the Sun Dance imparts). I believe I am being called to my second Sun Dance. Maybe next summer solstice, I must dance. It's not an easy time for me on my Sun Dance path, I'm afraid. And it's going to get harder soon. . . . The true story about Sun Dance is that the hardship comes much harder I think after the dance than during.

You may not know where you fit in or how to behave after you have made changes in your life. You will be returning to a life that has not caught up with you yet and that may not want to. You will need more courage on your return to carry you through than when you took the very first step. Is there anything more uncomfortable than a suit that pulls across the shoulders, with sleeves that are too short and pants that bind you everywhere? That may be how you will feel if you try to cram yourself back into your old world as if nothing has changed. It is no longer a question of surviving but of maintaining and thriving.

■ STORY: THE OTHER SIDE OF PAIN ■

Rachel's father was thirty-three when he took his own life. It happened a few days after her tenth birthday, and that was the last time she saw him. For twenty-three years she carried the pain of that loss and the unresolved questions, a ten-year-old's confusion as to her fault for his suicide. She carried the burden of her father's pain. Rachel had always dreaded her birthday, and the energy around the date was heavy and depressing. Rachel told me that she was afraid she might not live through her thirty-third year if she did not do some healing. To carry her further, she needed to find something significant and organic that traditional therapy had not included.

Rachel had chosen a career as a social worker and explained to me that it had been healing in many ways because she had to learn how to create boundaries and not take on other people's pain. At thirty-two, Rachel was married and had a child. She knew that she wanted to release her pain and her father's, create space for joy, and not pass the legacy and burden of pain onto her daughter. She asked friends for help, and together they designed a pagan-based ritual for letting go. Rachel's birthday was chosen as the date for her rebirth ceremony. They created an altar for objects representing what Rachel wanted to save relating to all the good memories of her father. She had loved her father a great deal and wanted to hold on to those strong, happy connections. They burned representations of the emotions and pain she wanted to let go in a big fire and sang and told stories. They celebrated Rachel's courage and her father's life.

The ritual was a life-altering experience for Rachel. Surrounded by friends and connecting to the pain organically with her voice and heart, she felt safe enough to let go. Pain this deep does not ever go away completely. We hope we can put it somewhere that it does us less harm. Rachel celebrates her birthday now and identifies with the significance of the day she was born.

■ EXERCISE: CREATING SACRED SPACE ■

On your return, challenges will be everywhere, from others and from within. Everything may appear familiar, but you can't return to the same place you left.

Creating sacred space is a reorientation of ourselves in the world. Sacred space exists in intimate moments when energy is clear and focused. You can create the same intensity in places you live and work. The key is your intention.

Create sacred space for yourself to retreat to and call upon for emotional strength and safety. Create a place of remembrance of why you wanted to make the changes in the first place. Sacred space is not found only in natural settings, outdoors, or in nature. Sacred spaces are not only physical places or ones that exist through legend. Sacred spaces already exist all around us; we need only to illuminate them.

Creating sacred space goes far beyond customizing your office or home with photographs and icons. Although they do have energy, that is changing merely the physical, unless you energize the atmosphere in and around these spaces and things.

Be clear about your dreams and hopes for the place you are creating. Be deliberate in your choices for the space and the energy you devote to it when you are there. If we let go of the daily pursuit of power over others and situations, but instead look to partner with others and the universe, we can create sacred space. Use all of your senses and focused energy to make a place of your own, whether it is a corner in a room or a place in your mind.

RESURRECTION

■□■□■□■□■□■□■□■□■□■□■□■□■□■□■□■■

You are not the person you were before if you have initiated even simple changes in your life. You have changed and may not be comfortable in your own skin. Not only that, but there will be temptations to return to the old ways of acting and reacting at every turn. Stay focused on where you are and where you want to go. Physically and spiritually put yourself in circumstances that support the changes you have made and the direction you are traveling. Keep a low profile for a while if that will ease your mind and spirit. If you come on big and strong before you have become fully comfortable with your transitions, you are just putting yourself out there like a big ol' saguaro cactus for the birds (family, friends, society) to peck away at. Come on out of the desert, chew these shifts slowly, and give yourself time for digestion.

▪ THE OLD NEIGHBORHOOD ▪

When you go back to your old neighborhood where you grew up, you may notice that everything seems smaller and maybe shabbier somehow. It doesn't take away from the important place it has in your history and on your journey, but it probably doesn't feel like home anymore. It is the same for a life before change. Returning or trying to is challenging now that you are in your new mind and in your new spirit. This is your unfolding and revelation, but now without the old crutches. At this final threshold you are using new sources of courage and perseverance to push through the unmasking. This is the time to find people who are traveling down the same road, who will support your efforts. Now is the time to nurture new sources of community and look for a new neighborhood to hang out in.

People will naturally appear in your life as you get involved with new activities and spend time in new places, and as your energy shifts. The energy you are putting out has changed, so what and who you attract will shift also. You may want to seek out new community, people who understand and support your choices. It will help keep you from slipping backwards. Rebirth is challenging, and digesting and assimilating subtle and grand change is part of this process. Your final exam is to show the world what you know now, and a cheering section of supportive fans is always good to have around.

People from your life will be pulling you back at the same time you are struggling with questions of your own identity and place in the world. It is possible that you may have to temporarily or permanently let go of one or several relationships that no longer support your efforts to move ahead. This is not an easy task to accomplish. Be assured, no one will let you go quietly. You may have acted as each other's cover or co-conspirator in self-destructive behavior. You may have given each other permission to avoid looking at the truth. If you are moving on, where does that leave them? If they are not ready to make changes in their lives, they certainly are not going to want you to. Relationships have to end sometimes, or at least be redefined for everyone's sake.

Resurrection can occur after coming through a challenging emotional situation and responding in a different way than you have before. It can be profoundly rattling and enlightening. It is likely that some of the behavior patterns you are breaking have been a part of you for a long time, if not your whole life. Put yourself in situations that support your transformation. Stay away from any that don't. As a newly sober friend of mine wisely said, "I guess I won't be hanging out in bars anymore." Beware of old habits trying to rear their big ol' loud heads at every turn.

It is never too late to push and pull ourselves out of the mud and not only choose a new road but head down it with some degree of confidence. Eleanor Roosevelt told us we must do what we fear most. I don't think that necessarily means you have to parachute out of an airplane if you have a fear of heights. It is changing the energy around the fear that involves faith at its highest level. There is a chance we may fail, but somewhere in our deepest selves is the image that we are capable and up to the task—that no matter what, we will be okay. The more we take risks with our spirits, and our hearts, the more we push our bodies, the greater the reservoir of strength we will have to call upon when we need it. The louder voice may have been saying for months, even years, "You are not ready, good enough, strong enough," etc. And then finally you will be able to listen to the smaller but more powerful voice coming from within, telling you that you will be supported in your efforts. All efforts are triumphs.

■ STORY: IN YOUR NEW SKIN ■

I have a Reiki client who quit smoking after thirty years. She came to me and asked for help, not with the physical addiction but with the psychological and emotional aspects that were making her frustrated. She had in fact dealt with the physical addiction quite easily. She was having trouble being resurrected as a non-smoker. It did not fit the image she had carried of herself for so many years. She wasn't going to take breaks to go out and smoke with her friends at work anymore, sit in the smoking sections in restaurants, or buy cigarettes from the same store once a week. These patterns had been a part of her life for so long, it was all a part of the physical habit of smoking, of her life as a smoker. Being a smoker was only one tiny piece of who she was, but for her it had become the focus and clearest self-image in her mind. Her physical realm has been impacted by the absence of cigarettes, and she can breathe easier. She has also become very interested in alternative healing and is exploring new spiritual paths. She is in some conflict with the doctrine and religion she was raised with and has questions about her own beliefs. Her spiritual world is the area I encouraged her to explore. The realm of the spiritual is where many of her questions lie and where she has found peace and strength in the past. This is the area of her life she feels capable of exploring and making energy shifts in that will impact her vision of herself.

■ EXERCISE: COMPLEMENTARY CHANGES ■

This week when you are doing three things that you have been meaning to get to, think of things that fit your shifts in energy and focus. If the more confident you is emerging, do something to support it. Now is the time to complement the changes you have initiated in other areas of your life. Now is the time to start the exercise program or ask a few people to meet you for dinner or a walk. Sign up for the class on comparative spirituality or attend the lecture by a local author. It is a good time to build a new support group for the new you, to keep you on track and feeling strong. You may want to find a club or group to join that takes you in a new direction with new people. Make regular time commitments, once a week or once a month. Keep the momentum building. Energy shifts will bring new people into your life, which will in turn impact your energy. You need to have the courage to ask them to be part of your world, and see what happens.

Autobiography in Five Chapters

1.
I walk down the street.
There is a deep hole in the sidewalk
I fall in.

I am lost . . . I am hopeless.
It isn't my fault.
It takes forever to find a way out.

2.
I walk down the same street.
There is a deep hole in the sidewalk.
I pretend I don't see it.
I fall in again.
I can't believe I am in the same place.
But it isn't my fault.
It still takes a long time to get out.

3.

I walk down the same street
There is a deep hole in the sidewalk.
I see it is there.
I still fall in . . . it's a habit.
My eyes are open.
I know where I am.
It is my fault.
I get out immediately.

4.

I walk down the same street.
There is deep hole in the sidewalk.
I walk around it.

5.

I walk down a different street.

■ □ ■

from the *Tibetan Book of Living and Dying*
—Translated by Sogyal Rinpoche

ASSESSMENT

■□■□■□■□■□■□■□■□■□■□■□■□■□■□■□■□■□■□■

So, here you are. Take a look at what has changed in your intimate world and beyond in the larger one. How do you feel? Is it how you want to feel? Now you have come full circle in the process. You will be in a different place from where you began. Take some time to have a look. Hopefully, you are arriving with greater clarity and confidence and feel better equipped to handle change in your life. Now it is time to jump off and initiate further momentum. The momentum is there to carry through for other changes to begin, and now you know how to make it happen. Changes will have happened, and there will be more decisions to be made in response and in the future. Once again we need to take an honest, thoughtful look at where we are—our truth.

■ WHAT HAPPENS NEXT? ■

At the end of this cycle of change, your small world and the larger have been forever altered. There will always be more to do, but you will never return to exactly the place you were before. There has been movement. There has been change. Resolutions in some areas will lead to questions and possibly more obstacles in another. Now you can use the momentum you have built to make other changes in your life and keep the process going. How far have you come and how far do you have to go? Goals and plans should be fluid and flexible. The world is changing at the same time, and you are not necessarily headed in the same direction or at the same speed. Carry your new truth into the day and see where you want to head next. Hopefully, this journey has sparked your curiosity and confidence in exploring your energy and interaction with the world. I imagine it hasn't always been easy to look at the truth, but maybe an appreciation for our individual and collective energy impact has been aroused. Maybe we can see one another "whole against the sky" and better appreciate the struggles of our fellow travelers.

■ STORY: ARE YOU TALL ENOUGH FOR THIS RIDE? ■

A friend of mine taught me that expression from his growing up, and it has stayed with me as a metaphor for facing new fears and challenges. It must come from the days when in order to ride the roller coaster at amusement parks, you had to be a minimum height. There is usually a marker line or a piece of wood nailed to a post, and your head had to reach that mark or no ride. I picture a group of pals heading off for an adventure and getting up enough courage to take their first ride, stepping up to the marker one after another before giving the attendant their tickets. And finally coming to the smallest in the group, whose head won't brush the marker even if he stands on his toes. Can you imagine his courage and excitement being shattered when the man says to him, "I am sorry, son, but you aren't tall enough for this ride." He knew he was tall enough for the ride on the inside. He was afraid but ready and willing to choke back his fears to give it a go, but he was denied the chance.

Don't let others decide for you if you are tall enough for the ride. Whether it is a new relationship, project, opportunity, or confrontation, you can use this question to judge your emotional, physical, and spiritual wellness before diving in or walking away. You have to make the determination yourself. Sometimes you know it immediately. If you have fear simmering inside, but are willing to go ahead and let it act as a catalyst rather than a burden, then you are tall enough and ready to ride. The friend who told me the expression went on to describe his first time going to the carnival that came through town every summer. He was pretty little. There was no roller coaster but some rickety rides that involved being shut in metal cages and thrown into the air without seat belts or any restraints. He decided he may not have been tall enough for that ride when after being flung around inside the cage for what seemed like an eternity, a bee flew in with him to really make it challenging. He emerged banged up and rattled and knew that one time was enough for that particular adventure, but he still knew he was ready.

Bees will fly into your ride when you think you have conquered all of your fears, or at least quieted them enough to make a move. Fasten your seat belt and expect the unexpected, because it will be along shortly. Obstacles in your path force you to figure out a way around them. And layers of obstacles, well, they just force you to figure a way out and around, over and over. It is all part of the journey, so you might as well go along with it. As my sister taught me about running and so in life, "It doesn't matter how fast you go as long as you keep going."

■ EXERCISE: JUST BE ■

You are well-loved and supported on your journey.

OVER PART

My sister and brother and I would do anything to get to stay up just a little bit longer when we were small. If we were parked in front of the television in our footie pajamas, we would beg to see what we called "the over part." The over part was the wrap-up piece of a TV show just after the last commercial. The show came back on for just a few minutes and either set you up for next week or tidied up the loose ends for that episode. I am not sure what you are getting with this "over part," but I will at least try and tie up any unruly thoughts and send you on your way.

We can stomp, grind, and fling energy into a space or settle and gently nudge it in. Either way, it will mix with all that already exists there. Simply, we are energy, and energy is all around us in every space we occupy. Our thoughts and dreams have mighty energy, too. Realizing desires just takes focus, putting them first. The words we choose to use and how we hold them inside are truly powerful. We bring our fears, hopes, love, and anger with us across every threshold. Our emotions and intentions are imposed upon or offered to the space and all that is present. This is the energy we are bringing. We are the state of mind and state of heart we bring to all that we do and everywhere that we roam.

The energy we give off and surround ourselves with is indeed what we attract and get back. Gaining awareness and understanding is the first little giant step toward change. You just have to decide where you want to go and how you want to get there. After all of your life experiences and tribal imprinting, how are you in the world? Has your authentic self been realized and revealed, or is it still hidden in a box under your bed?

Each and every day we need to make time and space to be alone in silence. Whether you choose to meditate, pray, reflect, or just be, find moments that are yours alone and that are quiet. Make the time when you first wake up, on your walk to work, in the shower, or before you fall asleep, to connect with quiet, conscious intention. Give thanks for all that you are and all that you have. Ask for guidance through difficult times, and look for the strength to make changes. It is easy to blame others for preventing shifts in our lives, but in fact you are the only one standing in your way.

We need to remind ourselves of what we are most grateful for, what makes our hearts full to bursting, and what actions and thoughts of ours require attention and scrutiny. Find a way to connect with nature or animals or people you love every day—whatever keeps you in balance and in gratitude. Challenge yourself physically to even out the energy whirling in your head and heart. Look at the world from a new perspective, tap into your creative self, and allow yourself to color outside the lines.

You will be supported by energy you may not be able to see but that is accompanying you at every step. It may not keep you from getting hurt; part of the process usually means letting go, making your energetic load a little lighter to carry. It is important to identify where it is that you want to go, what heights of spiritual transformation you want to achieve. Hold on to these visions but start from a place of truth, painful as that may be. Remember to come back to the thoughts that bring you joy, for therein lies clarity and strength. Make space for it in your head and heart and in your every day. Now look for the light. It may be tiny and far off—that is just how far you have to go. It will be an amazing journey. Off you go now.

BIBLIOGRAPHY

Ackerman, Diane. *A Natural History of the Senses*. New York: Vintage Books, reprinted edition, 1991.

Chardin, Pierre Teilhard de. "The Evolution of Chastity" from *Towards the Future*. New York: Harcourt Brace, 1973.

Cherry, Kelly. *Natural Theology—Poems by Kelly Cherry*. Baton Rouge, La.: Louisiana State University Press, 1988.

Dillard, Annie. *Mornings Like This: Found Poems*. New York: HarperCollins Publishers, 1995.

Ehrlich, Gretel. *The Solace of Open Spaces*. New York: Penguin Books, 1985.

Gandhi, M. K. *All Men Are Brothers: Life and Thoughts of Mahatma Gandhi as Told in His Own Words*. World Without War Publishing, 1972.

Jung, Carl Gustav. Herbert Read, ed. *The Archetypes and the Collective Unconscious (Collected Works of C. G. Jung, Vol. 9, Part 1)*. Princeton, N.J.: Princeton University Press, 1981.

Kalman, Tibor. A retrospective of his work. San Francisco Museum of Modern Art. 1998.

Lamott, Anne. *Tender Mercies, Some Thoughts on Faith*. New York: Pantheon, 1999.

Maslow, Abraham Harold. *Religions Values and Peak Experiences*. New York: Penguin USA, 1994.

Mitchell, Stephen, editor and translator. *The Selected Poetry of Rainer Maria Rilke*. New York: Vintage International, 1989.

Olsen, W. Scott and Scott Cairns, eds. *The Sacred Place*. Utah: University of Utah Press, 1996.

Rinpoche, Sogyal. Patrick Gaffney and Andrew Harvey, eds. *The Tibetan Book of Living and Dying*. New York: HarperCollins, 1993.

Ryan, Regina Sara. *The Woman Awake: Feminine Wisdom for Spiritual Life*. Arizona: Hohm Press, 1998.

St. John. Kieran Kavanaugh and Otilio Rodriguez, translators. *The Collected Wor* *of St. John of the Cross*. Washington, D.C.: ICS Publications, 1979, 1991.

Von Oech, Roger. *A Whack on the Side of the Head: How You Can Be More Creative* New York: Warner Books, 1992.

Williams, Terry Tempest. Robin Dresser, ed. *An Unspoken Hunger: Stories from the* *Field*. New York: Vintage Books, 1995.

ks

CREDITS

■□■□■□■□■□■□■□■□■□■□■□■□■□■□■□■■□■

Credits

Page 47: "To Live in Two Worlds," from *The Solace of Open Spaces* by Gretel Ehrlich, copyright © 1985 Gretel Ehrlich. Used by permission of Viking Penguin, a division of Penguin Putnam, Inc.

Page 147: Reprinted by permission of Louisiana State University Press from *Natural Theology*, by Kelly Cherry. Copyright © 1988 by Kelly Cherry.

Page 157: "Sonnets to Orpheus," from *The Selected Poetry of Rainer Maria Rilke* by Rainer Maria Rilke, translated by Stephen Mitchell, copyright © 1982 by Stephen Mitchell. Used by permission of Random House, Inc.

Page 171: "Autobiography in Five Chapters" [pp.171-72] from *The Tibetan Book of Living and Dying* by Sogyal Rinpoche and edited by Patrick Gaffney & Andrew Harvey. Copyright © 1993 by Rigpa Fellowship. Reprinted by permission of HarperCollins Publishers, Inc.